THE HARD JOURNEY HOME

THE HARD JOURNEY HOME

Real-Life Stories About Reentering
Society After Incarceration

The Think Outside the Cell Series

Edited by Sheila R. Rule and Marsha R. Rule

RESILIENCE
MULTIMEDIA

For information about this title or to order other books and/or electronic media, contact the publisher:
Resilience Multimedia
511 Avenue of the Americas, Suite 525
New York, NY 10011
www.thinkoutsidethecell.org
877-267-2303

ISBN: 978-0-9791599-3-0
Printed in the United States of America
Cover and interior design: 1106 Design

Please note: The image used on the cover is being used for illustrative purposes only. The man depicted is a model. (Photo: iStockPhoto.com)

For Joe

Contents

ACKNOWLEDGEMENTS

F irst, I am deeply grateful to the contributors, whose clear-eyed honesty, talent, and passion have made working on this book an incredibly satisfying experience.

My heartfelt appreciation to the Ford Foundation, whose generous support made publication of the *Think Outside the Cell Series* possible. I am forever grateful to one of the foundation's program officers, Calvin Sims, for ensuring that the voices of the incarcerated, the formerly incarcerated, and their loved ones are heard.

And for being there for me—always—I thank my family: my mother, Versa Rule; my sisters, Marsha and Diana; my nieces, Michaela and Alana and, of course, my son, Sean. I am thankful, too, that I had such a wonderful father; his compassionate heart continues to guide me.

A big hug to Kathleen McElroy for her sharp editing skills and loving embrace of the stories in this collection.

Finally, I thank Joe, who has given me so many reasons to be grateful to be in God's grace.

—Sheila R. Rule

I am deeply grateful to Sheila Rule and Joseph Robinson for their tremendous vision of creating a venue where the voices of the incarcerated and the formerly incarcerated can be heard, again and again and again.

I want to thank the authors of this collection for the gift of their stories and for reminding me of the interconnectedness of all of our lives.

And, of course, my great appreciation to all the wonderful relationships in my life!

—Marsha R. Rule

INTRODUCTION

The United States is the land of the imprisoned. With more than two million people behind bars, it is the leading jailer in the world. A policy of mass incarceration, one that rejects the value of rehabilitation and views crime and punishment through a distorted racial lens, has locked away more people than at any other time in this nation's history.

The members of this huge population are largely forgotten. Their voices are typically silenced behind prison walls, and loved ones and advocates who work on their behalf are given scant respect. When society considers them at all, it is as the faceless statistics or frightening stereotypes in which the media conveniently package them. They are defined by their mistakes and bad choices.

Approximately 700,000 of these men and women will be released this year. When they return to their communities throughout America, the long and uncompromising shadow of their incarceration will follow them. That shadow will so dramatically obscure their humanity that their hope of getting the support needed to successfully reintegrate into society and build meaningful lives will be tantamount to wishful thinking.

The shadow will follow them as they search for employment. Getting and keeping a job is one of the chief reasons a person avoids the revolving door of recidivism, yet employers routinely refuse to hire workers with criminal records.

The shadow will be there, too, when the formerly incarcerated seek stable and affordable housing, another critical building block for successful reintegration. Some private landlords simply won't rent to anyone with a record, and many others require what the formerly incarcerated often do not have—a history of good credit, stable employment, and successful rental experience. And for millions of people with prison in their past, certain laws make public housing and other assistance off limits. Some of the fundamental activities enjoyed by American citizens can be off limits, too, including the right to vote.

Another main component of successful reintegration revolves around healthy social networks and family support. But the long shadow crosses into the lives of loved ones, too. The incarceration of a family member who was a breadwinner can tip the balance in an already precarious financial situation, making the hard struggle for everyday survival that much harder. And the joy of a family member's return from prison—if the prison experience hasn't irretrievably severed family ties—can be tempered by worries over how to feed and clothe him until he gets back on his feet, if he ever does.

These and other policies, practices, and circumstances conspire to create the building blocks of modern-day inequality, crippling not only those who have spent time behind prison walls but also their families, their children, and the communities to which the formerly incarcerated return. In the end, society as a whole is damaged.

And perhaps cruelest of all, the long shadow can cast great self-doubt, leading those with prison in their backgrounds to give up on their most valuable asset—themselves.

The best hope for changing this situation lies in the larger society—from the next-door neighbor and church member to corporate America and government policymakers. They must listen to the voices of the incarcerated, the formerly incarcerated, and their families. When they listen, they will hear moving words of struggle, honesty, self-awareness, transformation, and hope. They will hear words that will change their opinions and crush long-held stereotypes, words that can help to lift the shadow.

Such words are in the pages of *The Hard Journey Home: Real-Life Stories about Reentering Society after Incarceration*.

The idea for this book had its roots in volunteer work that I began nearly a decade ago, after joining the Prison Ministry of the Riverside Church, a New York church internationally recognized for its commitment to social justice. I was asked to correspond with incarcerated men and women who wrote to the organization. And so I did.

Although generally dehumanized and demonized, the people I came to know through letters were multidimensional, complex human beings. More than a few were skilled and talented in a range of disciplines, from art and music to sociology, business, and the law. And many had used their time in prison to rethink and disavow the values and belief systems that had brought them there.

The people I came to know were much greater than the bad choices they'd made. And they so inspired me that I would eventually found a publishing company that, as part of its mission, would seek to present a more balanced view of the incarcerated through books that would allow them a voice and help them tackle some of the hard challenges they face.

My husband, Joseph Robinson—whose imminent and successful return from prison I pray for every morning—helped to give definition and structure to my book idea. He suggested that I develop a series of books that portray the realities, gifts, and diversity of experiences of people with prison in their backgrounds. The series would take its name from the title of the book he wrote several years ago to help people currently or formerly in prison to use their innate gifts to build successful lives: *Think Outside the Cell: An Entrepreneur's Guide for the Incarcerated and Formerly Incarcerated.* Other books in the *Think Outside the Cell Series* include *Love Lives Here, Too: Real-Life Stories about Prison Marriages and Relationships* and *Counting the Years: Real-Life Stories about Waiting for Loved Ones to Return Home from Prison.*

Contributors to *The Hard Journey Home* come to the issue of reentry in their own way. Larry White gives an intimate and honest account of his return to society after thirty-two years in prison: "I was seventy-three years old and alone... In those early months after coming home, I had only two dependable companions. One was loneliness. It sets in quietly in prison, and you accept it. But on the streets, it's palpable. The other companion was fear. I was scared to death of life on the outside. After all, coming home had been unexpected. I'd prepared myself to die in prison. I'd made my peace with it."

In Delores Mariano's first minutes beyond prison's gates, it is joy that is palpable: "The air on this side seems so much fresher. The trees—yes, trees—that we don't have behind the walls are still alive and well. Flowers! Oh, and a hug that I can have from my friend who's picking me up that is not limited to five seconds, like in the visiting room. I am free, free, FREE! It hits me with a jolt of reality; I am not behind the walls, not stuck in a twelve-by-eight hospital room anymore. This is life, this is reality, and this is the real world."

Deportation adds a harsh burden to Esther Morales Guzman's life on the outside: "I was in Tijuana, but with my daughter in the U.S., I became desperate. I felt my heart tighten. What good was my freedom if I couldn't be with her? I had to settle for talking to her on the phone. I needed to earn more money so that she could be with me. I wanted to get another job in the afternoons at the shelter where I was staying. The director agreed; but when she found out I was just out of prison, she took the job away."

As Tion Terrell compellingly explains, the customs adopted in prison in order to survive can make success on the outside an iffy proposition: "I started working at a construction company the next day. The environment was lax. I was eager to learn, and I worked hard. I was fired within two weeks for having too sharp a tongue with the crew's foreman. *In prison you always speak your mind or people will see you as a pushover. Then they'll try to victimize you.*"

Tariq Mayo lets readers in on his sometimes humorous thoughts about a recently released man's swift return to prison: "He just left here eighty-five days ago. Eighty-five days? That's 2,040 hours. Go 'head; do the math. I'll wait. That's eleven state movies. That's six commissary buys. In fact, it's still the same season it was when he left. I still have deodorant I bought when he was here."

For Melvin Wright, the death of his girlfriend casts a blinding light on the unbending rules and regulations—and unbending people—that can make the return home that much harder: "Finally, the day of Naomi's funeral rolled around.... It was then that I learned her mother had requested that she be buried in the family plot in New Jersey....New Jersey was another state and was definitely out of bounds for me. I decided to call my P.O. on her cell phone....I felt sure that everything would be all right since I'd kept her informed of my every move....As soon as I walked into her office, a male P.O. standing there told me to turn around and place my hands behind my back. He then put handcuffs on me...."

Dean A. Faiello offers lessons to fellow incarcerated men about the power they have to rise phoenix-like and stride back into society wiser, better, capable of building meaningful lives: "I wrote a seemingly incongruous list of names on the black-board—Nelson Mandela, Viktor Frankl, St. Paul, and Martin

Luther King, Jr. As I wrote the last name, the din began to subside. Dr. King often had that effect. I turned to face the class. 'Each of these men has something in common with the others. Anybody know what it is?' The classroom quieted down more as the guys realized they didn't have the answer."

By sharing the real stories of their lives, contributors to *The Hard Journey Home* offer lessons to us all. They are lessons that can help to create a more informed, compassionate, and just society—one story at a time.

—*Sheila R. Rule*
Publisher
Resilience Multimedia
September 2010

Larry White

From Reentry to Reintegration

After thirty-two years behind prison walls, I headed for life on the outside. I had forty state-issued dollars and the scrapbooks I'd filled over the years with pictures of places I dreamed of going, people I dreamed of meeting, and things I dreamed of doing.

But once I returned to New York City, where I found myself going most often was to a park bench. I would sit there gazing at the Hudson River and wondering how I would ever make it in society. I was seventy-three years old and alone. Both my wife and mother had died while I was in prison. My son lived in North Carolina; parole regulations barred me from visiting him. Another relative lived in New York, but visiting her would also have been a parole violation—I wasn't allowed near guns, and she was a police officer and kept guns in her home.

Like most long-timers, I didn't know anyone in the "legitimate society" that I was now expected to embrace and thrive in. All I knew was the 'hood and prison, which was an extension of the 'hood. How would I ever be able to connect with any of the mainstream people whom I'd been calling "squares" all my life? How was I now to become one of them?

In those early months after coming home, I had only two dependable companions. One was loneliness. It sets in quietly in prison, and you accept it. But on the streets, it's palpable. The other companion was fear. I was scared to death of life on the outside.

After all, coming home had been unexpected. I'd prepared myself to die in prison. I'd made my peace with it. I was denied release by the parole board four times; when I would appear at my scheduled hearings, the commissioners who held my fate wasted little time projecting an attitude that said, "Don't even sit down; you don't need to bother." I concluded that despite whatever I had accomplished in prison, I would keep getting denied because of the nature of my crime. I had been sentenced to twenty-five years to life for a murder and robbery. And not long after my arrest, while I was still in jail at Rikers Island, I had attempted to escape. I was captured in the East River. I was lucky; others who escaped with me drowned.

As I settled into years behind bars, I created a life that had meaning. I became a scholar. I started classes and programs, including those for men sentenced to life without the possibility of parole. I encouraged other incarcerated men to study their situation in the context of racism and this nation's history; it is no accident that the overwhelming majority of people in New York prisons are black and Latino and come from only a handful of poor neighborhoods in New York City. I organized the men to work to change prison conditions from inside and to stand up against disrespectful treatment at the hands of guards and corrections administrators. I organized them to own their power. Over time, this push for socially conscious empowerment became a movement that spread from one correctional facility to another in the state.

I reached a point in life where the only hard part about growing old in prison was my concern that I would someday be unable to protect myself against men with a predatory nature. But one day, a corrections officer urged me to try for parole one more time. He figured I might have a better shot at it now that the new governor, Eliot Spitzer, was ushering in what seemed to be a fairer approach to criminal justice than that of his predecessor, George Pataki. So, I gave it a try. And I was granted release.

As I whiled away hours on that park bench, I wondered if I'd made a mistake. I actually wanted to go back to prison.

It's not that I didn't have the basics that are critically needed upon release. I did. The Fortune Society, a nonprofit organization that promotes successful prisoner reentry, had thrown me a lifeline with housing, employment, medical care. For that, I was and remain deeply grateful.

But reentry is only part of the journey. Hundreds of thousands of people in this nation leave prison and reenter society every year, and far too many are doomed to be trapped in recidivism's revolving door. Why? Because they don't *reintegrate* into society. While they're warned against associating with the same old people in the same old neighborhoods that led them to prison, they are not equipped with the tools to make new, supportive connections; they don't know how to build new social networks and embrace a legitimate lifestyle. And they don't know where to turn in order to learn.

I counted myself among them. Yet, I knew I needed to reintegrate. And I wanted to—deeply. I wanted to become an active member of a community and raise my voice on issues that affected it. I wanted to participate in a range of social and cultural activities. I wanted to become a valued member of advocacy groups whose concerns reflected my own. I wanted to belong.

At some point, I took a deep breath and tried to figure out reintegration for myself. I tentatively dipped my toe into the life of the city. I joined two other men who, like me, were newly released from decades-long prison sentences and made forays to a big supermarket not far from where we lived. We were accustomed to prison shopping—basically checking off items on a printed commissary list—and completely over-whelmed by the wide array of foods spread out before us at the supermarket. With our one cart, the three of us would mainly just stand and gawk, so much so that a store manager once asked us if there was a problem.

I would take the subway here and there. At first, I was so self-conscious that I thought everyone was staring at me and thinking, "He just got out of prison." I would look down at the floor and literally break out in a cold sweat.

I started venturing to places in my scrapbooks. I love jazz, and I began attending lectures, movies, and rap sessions at the National Jazz Museum in Harlem. I always enjoyed myself, but I didn't know how to strike up a conversation with anyone. At the end of a museum event, I'd briefly watch with envy as others in attendance easily mingled with each other, and then I'd leave. But as I walked down the street after one event, I passed a woman who had been in the audience. She actually stopped me and started talking about how she'd enjoyed the event. It was a real conversation; it made me feel good. I began to think of other places I might go, other people I might meet.

In prison, I attended meetings sponsored by the Quakers. So, I found my way to the Quakers on the outside. Members invited me to dinner; they took me out. They helped me make connections. I had also followed and admired the work of the Prison Action Network (P.A.N.), an advocacy organization that works on behalf of the incarcerated and their families in New York State. I got involved with that organization and soon became one of its leaders, lobbying legislators, meeting with senior parole and corrections officials, and developing programs for the incarcerated. I even helped to draft legislation intended to help gain release for thousands of deserving incarcerated men and women in New York State who keep being denied because of the nature of their crimes.

My circle of contacts and friends grew ever wider. I created a supportive social network. I became part of a community.

When I walked out of prison, I told the men I left behind that I would not forget them. I told them that I'd be back.

And I have gone back, with programs, ideas, guidance, and support. I would feel lost if I couldn't be there for them, in one way or another. But as I head back to my new community at the end of a prison visit, I give thanks that I made it out alive.

Tion Terrell

My First Prison Education

On March 18, 1999, I was released from jail after serving a one-year sentence. I had nine years and twelve months suspended time over my head. I had no place to go. Because I could not be released without a home destination, I had a pen pal tell Department of Corrections officials that I would be living with her. It was a lie. My plan was to manipulate her into allowing me to take up permanent residence with her.

My grand plan was to work two jobs, save money, stay off drugs, and get my life together. The plan was a solid one, fully detailed and in writing. Plus, I had every confidence that I could talk myself into just about anything, and even out of most of the trouble I could get into.

My first disappointment came three days after my release. My pen pal told me I could not live with her. I turned to my aunt, the only family member I'd dare describe as stable. It took some emotional bullying, but I finally got her to agree to let me live with her temporarily. However, she set a condition that I knew beyond a shadow of a doubt she would enforce: I was never to be inside the house when she wasn't there.

She had good reason for this stipulation. Years earlier, while strung out on crack cocaine, I stole some expensive jewelry from her.

Her first words, after laying down all the ground rules, were, "You need to get a job." She even went as far as rambling off the names of places that she knew were hiring.

I activated my master plan. I started by obtaining emergency food stamps from social services. I gave them to my aunt to assist with grocery bills. An ex-con's first concern, if not sex, is to eat all the favorite foods he's been deprived of while incarcerated. He may do so gluttonously for a spell, and possibly at speeds that can only be described as doggy.

My first employment was at a temporary labor agency. I started within a week after my release. My workweek consisted of fifty-six hours—double shifts Mondays, Wednesdays, Fridays, and evening shifts on Tuesdays and Thursdays. I job-hunted on Tuesdays and Thursdays and during the day on weekends. I couldn't rest at home anyway.

In only a few weeks, I landed a full-time job and a steady part-time job. I also saved enough money to move into a rooming house. I was proud of myself. But I now realize I made a crucial mistake by not allowing myself time to adjust to society emotionally and psychologically before plunging head first back into it.

To explain why an appropriate adjustment period is so critical to an ex-con's success, I must describe what it means to be institutionalized. An institution is any established practice, law, or custom. Therefore, an institutionalized person is one who adapts to such a practice, law, or custom. Criminal delinquency is an institution in and of itself. It's psychopathic in that criminals hold little regard for the rights of others and are proud of their antisocial behavior. Convicted criminals are re-institutionalized by their incarceration. They are continuously subjected to activities like compulsive gambling, racketeering, extortion, theft, robbery, exploitations, drug addiction, the use of illegal and prescribed psychotropics, alcoholism, indecent exposure, assaults, rape, and even murders. These are all social norms in jails and prisons.

Because of these environmental norms, newly released prisoners should have at least a few weeks in a safe and healthy environment to adjust to the civilian lifestyle before taking on the stressful responsibilities of job seeking and financial independence.

In fact, the vast majority of ex-cons need some form of therapy to help them understand that the customs and practices adopted in prison are inappropriate and counterproductive in society. The adjustment period should be spent with people emotionally equipped to be patient with the ex-prisoner's unusual reactions to everyday circumstances that a relatively normal person would react more appropriately to, or perhaps would even ignore.

Here are cases in point, and the lessons learned:

My first full-time job was as a supervisor at a restaurant. Two weeks into my supervisory training, I noticed a customer waiting impatiently at the takeout window. The employees who manned that station were legitimately preoccupied, so I went over and took the customer's order. As I keyed in the order, something occurred in my work area that required my immediate attention. I returned to my area as soon as I finished taking the order at the takeout window.

"Hey, you gotta come make this," a young worker demanded at the station I'd just left.

"I'm busy right now," I said. "That's your station anyway. You make it."

He drew himself up—the way a gorilla would before beating its chest. "Nah, that ain't how it works 'round here. If you take the order, you make the order."

"That's your station," I replied. I was irritated. "I did you a favor by taking the order. I'm the supervisor. I'm asking you."

"I don't care what you is, nigga," he barked, cutting me off. "You don't tell me what to do. I'll fuck you up."

I immediately dropped what I was doing and started untying my apron as I approached the pugnacious youngster.

In prison, disrespect must be straightened out immediately.

The supervisor who was training me happened to be a woman. When she grabbed me from behind, I didn't resist for fear of injuring her. The next day I reported the incident to the general manager and explained that I was uncomfortable working around the insubordinate kid. The manager said he couldn't fire the young man, so I quit.

You can never take a threat lightly in prison, and you must never turn your back on an enemy.

I started working at a construction company the next day. The environment was lax. I was eager to learn, and I worked hard. I was fired within two weeks for having too sharp a tongue with the crew's foreman.

In prison, you always speak your mind or people will see you as a pushover. Then they'll try to victimize you.

I had a girlfriend by then, too. She cried when she learned I'd lost yet another job. She said she was falling in love with me, but that my instability was scaring her. To comfort her, I made promises, excuses, and rationalizations. I also gave her half of my last paycheck.

The most noticeable deprivation an inmate faces is interaction with members of the opposite sex. It's real easy to get sprung when you get out.

So it was back to the temp agency for me. I didn't mind. Most of my co-workers were drug addicts. They didn't take good care of themselves. Among them, I shined like a brand new quarter. I felt good comparing myself to them.

In prison, status is directly related to one's image. There is too little to feel good about when leading such a stagnant life. Self-esteem is usually based upon others' inadequacies. Very low expectations!

I had a reputation. My image was the same as it had been before I went to jail. So, people assumed I was back into the drug business. After a few solicitations from promising customers, I bought some crack at a wholesale price to distribute at a profit.

My girlfriend and I had little in common outside our sexual appetites. We'd been going through the motions without paying attention to who the other really was as a person. It just so happened that this reality hit us both right around the time I'd begun dealing drugs again. Our breakup was abrupt.

This was the single most devastating event of my life—at least that's how I felt at the time. The condition we loosely call "sprung" is clinically known as "dependent." I really believed my girlfriend completed me as a person—even though I didn't know her. We'd met within a week of my release and sex had occurred within days of our first meeting. I latched onto her with reckless abandon. All her whims took precedence over my legitimate needs.

I've since learned that no one can complete another person. We all must learn to be happy with ourselves and by ourselves. If we can't do this, no relationship will be a happy one for long because it will be plagued with unreasonable expectations and demands.

Having allowed myself to become dependent on her, the breakup left me broken, angry, lonely, hurt, and confused. I needed relief, an escape. I relapsed into crack cocaine.

In prison, instant gratification is always justified.

Five hours after my first hit, I still felt the same emotions. My high was crashing and I was broke. Rent was due. Worse, I was scheduled to meet with my P.O. in only a few days. The mandatory drug screening would test positive. Violation! Prison time!

I jumped off a bridge into the James River. I lived. DAMN IT!

After almost a week in the hospital, I moved back in with my aunt. Same rules applied. The next weekend was spent partying in the streets. I drank and smoked weed from Saturday morning until I reported to the temp agency Monday afternoon.

My aunt threw me out on Tuesday because I hadn't bothered to call home to let her know that I was okay.

I can't blame her. She had an impressionable young daughter whom she was raising by herself.

However, no one should be expected to go from being a delinquent, to a prisoner, to an upstanding, responsible, productive citizen. It simply isn't realistic. For most, the transition from prisoner to civilian is only a physical one. The ex-con is often more of a psychopath than when he entered prison. But the most frightening reality is the ex-con is probably not even aware of it.

Every criminal "knows" that cops, prosecutors, judges, correction officers, and parole officers are all crooked. They have no right to tell us what to do. They just want to control everybody. Ain't nothing wrong with getting over on the system, or on innocent people.

I moved in with a family of four after my aunt threw me out. I was sleeping with the woman of the house anyway. Of course, her boyfriend didn't know. Her kids were too young to be of consequence.

Gambling's a way of life in prison. If it feels good to you, you do it. Just don't get caught.

After a few months of searching, I found my dream job. It offered the potential for power, wealth, and prestige. My only boss was the owner of the restaurants we operated. I did what I wanted to do, including sleeping with employees.

Every prisoner wants to make up for lost time when it comes to sex.

My income from work wasn't enough. With benefits, I earned from $30,000 to $50,000. I still peddled drugs on the streets, and sometimes I gambled for extra cash.

Most of this money was spent on or with my greatest love. She was young, intelligent, and beautiful. She really had me sprung.

She often told me I wasn't quite right. I said things that were inappropriate. My behavior was erratic. I got angry too quickly. I acted as if violence was the answer to every problem. Plus, I smoked way too much weed. Despite my undying love for this woman, who's now estranged, I never listened to her.

You have to be your own man in prison. You're weak if you let others tell you what to do, or how. You can't care what nobody thinks.

My girlfriend got pregnant. Two other women were allegedly carrying my children, too. I was totally stressed out. I smoked even more weed in order to cope. Then, I lost my job.

I had to hustle full-time. I started using various drugs to hide from reality and sound thought. So, I submitted two urine samples that tested positive for drugs.

When I faced the judge after my probation was violated, he had some compassion for me and sent me to a halfway house.

I don't remember much about the halfway house. I know what I did while there though. I back-talked to staff, manipulated my work schedule to make time to sleep with different women, and I lied about my income, which enabled me to keep more money on my person than the rules allowed. I was kicked out in less than two months.

You ain't a "real nigga" if you ain't rebellious.

I'm back in prison now, and I'm disgusted with myself. When I observe my peers, I watch them learn the lessons I've mentioned here—the same lessons that brought me back to prison within a year of my release. I recognize the psychopathic tendencies my girlfriend saw in me. It's all very painful.

I agree with what the poet and educator Nikki Giovanni wrote in her essay, "Campus Racism 101":

> "What's the difference between prison and college? They both prescribe your behavior for a given period of time. They both allow you to read books and develop your writing. They both give you time alone to think and time with your peers to talk about issues. But four years of prison doesn't give you a passport to greater opportunities. Most likely that time only gives you greater knowledge of how to get back in."

I believe the worst part of prison life—second to the psychopathic institutionalization I've described—is the total lack of responsibility inmates enjoy. The institution provides all necessities, so inmates are enabled to loaf. Some obtain jobs and an education, but they are a minute percentage of the country's prison populace. Generally, convicts slide through their incarcerations on a free ride while often blowing their loved ones' money on frivolities and destructive ventures.

When I wrote this story, I had less than two years remaining on my sentence. Writing it forced me to evaluate the ways I've been reinstitutionalized by this sojourn, despite my being aware that it was happening. I'd already decided to turn my prison stay into my personal rehab. Self-help, academics, disciplined time management, and avoidance of frivolous and destructive discourses and behaviors have helped me to prepare for release and have alienated me, to a degree, from my peers.

At the same time, though, I've chosen vices. I'd lie by omission if I didn't admit that. We all get tainted in here.

I advise anyone who'll listen to learn from my experiences. Society is neither understanding nor tolerant. As citizens struggle to make their way in a highly competitive world, they'll run over, abuse, and scapegoat anyone they can. As convicted felons, we're easy targets. Institutionalized convicts might as well not leave prison's gates, because they'll soon return anyway—that is, unless they get the support and guidance they need upon release. For those convicts who willingly maintain their ignorance and counterproductive beliefs, they have no chance at all.

Epilogue

I've returned to society again, and I've found a cruel world.

I fell in love with a wonderful woman before my release, and I moved in with her upon leaving prison. We live in Collinsville, Illinois, in a predominantly white community. She lives on a fixed income, so I knew my challenges upon reentry would be many, despite my extensive managerial experience and my anticipated success as an author and poet. The world is more fraught with challenges than I anticipated. After my release, I struggled to acquire necessities, including a job, transportation, clothes, and a social network. Reentry assistance programs here in Madison County are limited. The few that I've found are for those on probation or parole, and don't apply to me. Most alarming of all is that, due to my indigence, I can't get mental health counseling while I adjust psychologically to society after almost ten years of incarceration—the last three of which were spent in segregation, which is known to induce psychological deterioration.

After many frustrations, I took my search for assistance to local and federal politicians; it's too soon to expect in-depth answers from busy elected officials in Washington, but some of their offices mailed me some information. On the local level, I started with my state representative; an assistant found a program that would help me, but only after I completed orientation and a three-day class. The program is in St. Louis, Missouri, a neighboring state. Bus fare would cost approximately $32. The state representative's office couldn't help me with that.

I called the mayor's office; I give Mayor John Miller credit for personally following up on my call. I talked to the City Clerk, who sent me to the Clerk of Courts. I called the City Board of Supervisors. The man I spoke with there referred me to the local Presbyterian church that sponsors a food pantry. I visited the church and was told about a thrift clothing program that would help me. I could also get help with transportation—once I found a job. The pastor said he wanted to see me helping myself. This was disconcerting—since I was trying to help myself—although it was understandable.

Still, where was I to get bus fare to search for work?

At some point, I was referred to the Department of Probation. I spoke with a friendly, delightful, and very helpful secretary there named Suzanne Johnson. Unfortunately, she could not work miracles and direct me to resource programs that are nonexistent. But she did tell me about two businesses that sometimes hire people with criminal records.

I called both businesses, but only reached someone at one, a restaurant. A man who identified himself as the co-owner told me to come in after 10:30 a.m. I got there at 11:00 and was told to come back at 3:00. This left me with time to kill and three dollars to my name. Going home and coming back would've left me broke.

So, I prolonged my job search. I visited several other restaurants, since this is where my experience lies. I also stopped at Township Hall and spoke with a nice woman named Marilyn who told me that she would speak with her supervisor about aiding me with a bus pass.

With time still left to kill, I went to the public library to get a library card, and to borrow some books. I was surprised at how busy the library was. When I commented on this to the librarian, he told me that the number of people borrowing books had increased lately.

A light bulb flashed on. I immediately asked him to call the publisher of the book in which you're reading my story, and we arranged two book signings featuring yours truly.

When those arrangements had been made, it was time for my three o'clock interview, which turned out to be a rejection before it even began. What was funny was that the owners hadn't even looked at my resume. I have great experience working at restaurants. I'm forced to wonder if my ex-con status blinded the owners to my skills, qualifications, and potential, after all.

It wouldn't surprise me. I've been the victim of prejudice of all types. One of my neighbors sent the police to question me after I gave her a note that suggested we could be friends. And, YES, that's all the note suggested. The crazy part is that the police even bothered to look into such a trifling complaint. Then again, I'm a black ex-con in a neighborhood where they feel I don't belong, and she is a young, attractive white woman.

Well, after leaving the pointless interview, I stopped by my state representative's office, where I met the assistant who'd told me about the program in St. Louis. Her lack of enthusiasm seeped through her pores. It seemed to me that she rated me and my problems as nothing more than a nuisance. I think I understand why, though. I hold no grudges.

She'd been told that reentry assistance is provided to Illinois prisoners before they are released. I told her she wasn't given the whole truth, and that state IDs, bus passes, clothes, and psychological debriefings were not provided.

She didn't seem to want to even consider that I might be telling the truth. Then I told her that a weaker man in my position would be considering criminal activity as a means of survival. She quickly warned me not to say such things. I think she thought I was making a threat.

As I write this, two of my problems have been solved, for now. I will pick up free clothing in a few days. Marilyn at Township Hall called a few hours ago to tell me that I would be given bus tickets to get me to and from the program in St. Louis.

Beyond that, I'm at a loss. Ms. Johnson at Probation has been working hard to find some answers, but that's not exactly good news. If she is a secretary in the Office of Probation and doesn't know how to help an ex-con find resources, such resources must be embarrassingly scarce.

I wonder if the recidivism and repeat-offender statistics are higher here than in other places.

The experience I've had reentering society forces me to make two points:

1. Prisons are warehouses that enable treatment counselors, psychologists, administrators, investors, and even some politicians to earn livings for doing nothing. Inmates aren't required, nor encouraged—and in some cases even allowed—to apply themselves. They are shuffled through programs so the conductors can meet their quotas. The policymakers get snow-jobbed—some of them willingly—about what is really happening. They get to pretend the system is working while the problem gets worse. The real crime is that the constituents' attention is diverted from the reality that spending on criminal justice increases while spending on public education decreases in the neighborhoods from which so many incarcerated people come.

2. Despite this, prisoners must work their absolute hardest and utilize every tool at their disposal to grow, change, and educate and prepare themselves before they return home. It's hard enough coming home with education, skills, and a positive can-do attitude. Imagine what it's like without them.

I've been labeled a "crusader" by those closest to me because of my determination to educate the public about this sad reality. The real truth is that, if we as individuals don't attempt to be part of the solution, we are all contributors to the problem.

Crime will spread. It can do nothing else.

The average person doesn't care about my struggle until someone like myself turns them or one of their loved ones into a victim. Then they are quick to point the finger of blame without comprehending that desperation, mis-education, and ignorance drive people to criminal activity—all of which are a direct consequence of our society's social and economic injustices.

So, now I've accepted the responsibility of making sure all the prejudiced finger-pointers are pointing at mirrors.

Bridget Jones

Journey Leading Nowhere

I slowly glance at the calendar on the wall. I will be released in less than ninety days. Who is going to help integrate me into the community? The report sent to Washington says Inmate 23063009 is rehabilitated and ready to enter society again. Am I?

The moment that every inmate looks forward to sends terror through my soul. I am homeless, jobless, have no family support, and no transportation. The only thing I will leave here with is hope. But as I look at the calendar, my hope becomes frustration. My frustration screams, "Where is the Second Chance Act for me and my babies?"

My two babies have been raised for the last year by church members, but they have loved me in spite of my mess. They are orphans while I am in prison. My children are depending on me to get a home and put our family back together again, but they do not understand that I have been working for only twelve cents an hour for the past year. They don't understand that Mommy has taken all the classes available to her, but there is still not a plan for our life.

I think back to the day of my sentencing and the judge declaring, "You owe me time." The amount of time to be served was decided and my debt to society was to be paid in full upon completion of my sentence. Why do I still feel as though it's never going to be enough? I have to give more every time "no one has time," each time my paperwork is not processed in a timely manner, or when the halfway houses are supposedly "too full" to accept me. Everyone can take from me because I messed up. I need someone to give back to my family and me.

The world is prejudiced against the new title now associated with my name and Social Security number—"felon." No job, no housing, and no opportunities equal no forgiveness. Citizens expect justice to be served on those who break the law. However, at what point does that justice become a lifetime of torture? Is the judgment ever enough to repay the debt owed for the offense?

I have to reenter this community whether or not prison has prepared me. Once my sentence expires, no one can make me stay. How I leave and the way the community receives me will make a difference in my success. Whether I try to make it the right way or the wrong way is up to me. But the types of programs and community support available matter to each prisoner. They have to work. If they are dead ends, I am back to where I started.

I have feelings of fear and rejection, knowing I need a second chance. I need someone to tell me and the thousands of others what we must do to get the tools to move forward! Will we be able to return home with greater hope for success if no one tries to make a difference in our transition back into society?

I stare at the calendar and watch time fly by. I look at a day spent here. My government pays for my housing, food, medical care, and employment. But, unfortunately, I am no closer to being ready to leave with skills or resources than I was the day I arrived.

My program review lists all the classes I have successfully taken. On paper, it may appear that I have all the resources to succeed. In reality, I am a fraud with fictitious reentry skills. The classes are taught by non-professionals without expertise or education, or on videos that require anywhere from one hour to six weeks to complete. A video titled *Pre-Release* was the tool I was given to succeed. Of course, taxpayers have been programmed to think that the system has helped me to acquire the tools I need to avoid recidivism.

The hard truth is that I am fighting for my family and me. My reentry is solely dependent on my faith that I can do this alone. No programs or resources in federal prison have proven to be worth the millions wasted on them or on the poorly educated staff. Prisoners' families help by mailing updated information, and, through the generosity of other inmates, we share resources.

Decades-old videos are not relevant. What matters to me is how I can find the resources I need to help my family and me succeed today.

Today I need and want a second chance. Today I am seeking resources to guide me away from reoffending. Before I know it, I will turn and look at this calendar and it will be the day I go home. I know I will be unprepared, and I will wonder why nobody prepared me yesterday for today's challenges.

Esther Morales Guzman

Crossing the Border for Eliza

I migrated to the United States in 1989 with my cousin and her husband. I arrived in Los Angeles. The situation was not as difficult then. I quickly purchased my fake paperwork in MacArthur Park to work in the United States. I started earning a good salary; I was working hard and saving money. During that time there was a lot of work. I would travel every year to Oaxaca, Mexico, and leave with enough to pay a coyote—a smuggler—between $300 and $350 for my return. I felt happy and fulfilled, especially because I was able to send money to my family.

In 1992 my mother died, and I felt very lonely. That's when I decided to have a baby. I returned to Oaxaca and sought out one of my friends from childhood. I had to smoke marijuana and drink alcohol because, although he was a handsome man,

I have always loved women and have known I am a lesbian for as long as I can remember. We had sex one time, and the following month I knew I was pregnant. I wanted a little girl.

I returned to Los Angeles. My pregnancy was very healthy and beautiful. On April 2, 1993, my dream was realized—my beautiful baby girl was born. I was thrilled and thanked God for her. Nothing mattered other than my daughter, Eliza, named in honor of my mother. She had all of my love and was the most important thing in my life.

We lived with my brother Luis and sister Silvia. They later moved out of the apartment, and Eliza and I were left alone. Being a single mother was very difficult. But Eliza and I kept on; we were an American family. I would leave Eliza with a babysitter during the day and pick her up in the afternoon. As she got older, I would drop her off at school and pick her up after school. Eliza was very happy, and so was I.

One day I purchased a DJ music system for Eliza's birthday parties and get-togethers with friends. We had a large patio with an avocado tree, where I put up a swing for my daughter and placed the music system during events. One Friday evening during one of these get-togethers, I tried cocaine for the first time. I felt happy with all my friends, and cocaine made me feel like a superwoman. It became a habit. Friday and Saturday we would party, and Sunday I would rest before work on Monday.

Eliza was seven years old, and I lived in a world of drugs. Three years passed, and I struggled with my addiction but remained in denial. My family started to realize my problem. I met my responsibilities and was a great mother to Eliza. I made sure that she had everything she needed, including my love and protection.

One Thursday, I gave Eliza permission to spend the night at her friend's house. My friends and I went to a bar, where we drank and bought cocaine. At some point, I felt an urge to leave; when I used drugs away from home I would panic and want to see my daughter. The woman who had bought the cocaine suddenly could not find her drugs. When I announced that I was leaving, she thought that I had stolen the cocaine. She fought with me.

I hurried to my truck, and the group followed me. They tried to destroy the truck and hurt me. I put the truck in reverse, not realizing that one of the women was behind the truck. I left, but two streets away, I was detained and arrested.

My life changed completely that Thursday. My daughter was left waiting for me at her friend's house. I was taken to jail, drugged and drunk, not realizing the tremendous situation I was in. My cousin traveled from San Jose to Los Angeles and picked up Eliza the next day because if she had not done so, the state was going to take her. My family turned their backs on me. My sister said I was in that situation because of my irresponsibility and my addiction. My family forgot about me.

I was accused of attempted murder and expected to receive a twelve-year sentence. I spent months in a Los Angeles County jail fighting my case, feeling like the worst being on earth, asking myself how I could have done something so horrible. The person I ran over did not die, but she could have. I wondered what was going to become of my daughter. I had destroyed our lives. I would sit in a corner with my mind lost.

I contemplated committing suicide. I could not stand having failed as a mother.

Then one day I began to receive letters that included these words: "You are the best mother on earth," "I love you so much," "Everything is going to be okay." I was embarrassed to write back, but the letters kept coming: "I'm doing fine," "I miss our home," "I'm going to start going to school." She would write, "I can't sleep," and include the time she was writing—"3:00 a.m." Her letters were killing me inside. She would ask, "When are you coming for me?" "I'm going to wait for you." "Mommy, I love you."

Months passed, and I was sentenced to five years in prison. I did not have the courage to tell Eliza. With my heart broken, I accepted my sentence.

One day I heard my name, "Morales," and I heard the sound of chains. I was very scared. That night I was transferred to prison, California Rehabilitation Center (C.R.C.) in Norco. I was chained from my hands to my waist and from my waist to my feet. When we arrived, I felt like a lion that had just been released from a small cage.

At first, everyone looked at me. I would not speak, much less smile. My heart agonized every day, and I asked for death to come. Everyone eventually ignored me, and I ignored everyone. The first year I shaved my head. It was the style in prison among lesbians. I worked hard in the kitchen area. I worked for twenty-six months, from 4:00 a.m. to 10:00 a.m. By that time, Eliza and I wrote to each other almost every day. Her letters made me smile again. I was able to run, jump, play, and to look around me and realize that not everything was lost. I wanted to hug someone. I began searching for friends.

In 2003 they closed C.R.C. and we were all transferred. I was sent to Valley State Prison for Women (V.S.P.W.). Again, fear began to creep up in me. This time I was ready. I knew that V.S.P.W. was a high-security prison. The move there was very intense. Again, I was chained, stripped naked, forced to bend down and cough, exposed to the terrifying flashlight, and had all of my body examined. It took six hours to get to V.S.P.W. I wished that instead of heading to another prison, I could go to Eliza.

When we arrived at V.S.P.W., I breathed in deep and thought, "Two more years." By this time I would just shave the bottom part of my head. In prison, there are two choices, the good path and the bad. I always followed the good path, even though my outer being—my shaved head and my baggy clothes—said something different. Time passed quickly. I found myself among beautiful women, laughs and cries, football and handball, and my art, including paper flowers, drawing, and jewelry making.

When I had thirty days left at V.S.P.W., I felt incredible. I even walked and breathed differently. I made a miniature card and sent it to Eliza, letting her know my last day in prison: June 7, 2008.

I was thrilled and at the same time afraid. I would go to bed wondering, "What am I going to do?" "Where am I going to go?" "I don't know anyone in Tijuana," where I was being sent. I had lived in Los Angeles for eighteen years and in prison for five. I imagined I would have to spend my nights at the bus station.

When the anticipated day came, I thought, "Freedom at last." My hair was growing back. But I knew that outside the prison gate, a monster was waiting for me—society. It began even before leaving prison. I did not qualify for the new clothes or nice shoes usually given to women leaving prison because I was undocumented. The other women who were leaving were so happy, with new clothes and $250 cash. I left with my gray clothes and without a cent in my pocket. A U.S. immigration agent eventually picked me up. I was transferred to the immigration office, where I signed a voluntary deportation form. Later I was taken to the airport in Fresno, where I joined other women who shared my fate. When the airplane arrived, the agents lined up all of us. Again, they chained our hands to our waists, and our waists to our legs, then loaded us on the airplane. I tried to get comfortable and put the seat back, but I was not allowed. Several agents lined up along the pathway looked at us as if we were animals. I thanked God that the trip was over quickly. When we arrived in San Diego, they took us to the immigration office. There we waited until 4:00 a.m. And then we were deported. The agents yelled, "Leave!" Several women screamed back at them.

I walked across the rails into Mexico. I didn't know where to go. Suddenly I heard a policewoman: "What are you doing, mami?" In that instant she grabbed and handcuffed me. This cannot be happening, I thought. She put me in a truck full of drunken men who smelled horrible. We were taken to the police station and made to line up. We were going to be fined for not having identification. I showed them my deportation paperwork and they let me go around 10:00 a.m.

I started walking without knowing where to go. I was very hungry. I walked for four hours, and then I suddenly remembered a television show that I had seen years before about a shelter for migrants. I was walking behind a stranger and asked him about it. He was very polite and explained how to get to a shelter. I was very embarrassed but asked him if he could give me money for the bus. He gave me the exact change, and I thanked him. But I took the wrong bus. Instead of going to La Postal, where the shelter is located, I took the Santa Fe bus. I asked strangers for directions, and I walked.

I was almost there when I came upon a pathway with many stairs that I would have to climb. I decided to rest for a moment underneath a tree. An older lady who was watering her plants started talking to me, and she took me into her house. I told her that I was very hungry and she gave me food. She even bought me a soda. By the time I left it was dark.

When I arrived at the shelter, I was assigned a bed, given some clothes, and was able to take a shower. I was so tired that I fell asleep as soon as I put my head on the bed. The next day I sat down on the patio and wondered what I was going to do. As I listened to everyone's story, the only things I heard discussed were coyotes, border crossings, and getting detained. I got up and left. When I walked past the house of the older lady who had helped me, I asked her where I could find a job not too far from there. She oriented me, and I left to look for work.

I did not find any work that day. To start from zero in an

unknown city takes a lot of work. The next day I looked for work again. This time, I found a job at a restaurant, where they tested my cooking skills and made me an assistant cook, working from 6:00 a.m. to 2:00 p.m. and getting paid about ninety dollars a week. As soon as I was able, I called Eliza, who was very happy to hear my voice. A lot of my money would go into calls I made to Eliza, but I was so happy.

One day I got to the shelter after work and saw a group of women eating chips and drinking soda. I asked if there was a party, and they said that a young lady had bought the snacks. I sat and ate with them. That young woman was interested in talking with me for her research project on migrant women, but I was rude to her. She wanted to hear my story. "What do I get out of it?" I asked. She was very nice and polite, and I eventually agreed to go with her to downtown Tijuana to talk about my experiences.

———◦◦———

Reintegrating into society is very difficult. I was simply not able to do it. Although I was free, I felt a terrible loneliness.

I was in Tijuana, but with my daughter in the U.S., I became desperate. I felt my heart tighten. What good was my freedom if I couldn't be with her? I had to settle for talking to her on the phone. I needed to earn more money so that she could be with me. I wanted to get another job in the afternoons at the shelter where I was staying. The director agreed, but when she found out I was just out of prison, she took the job away. I was very upset. What could I do here alone, without a home? I wanted to have my daughter here with me. I did not know what to do. Eliza would ask me about our future. I asked her to let me think things through. I saved some money and sent it to her for her passport, so that she could visit during her vacation. The thought of that visit made us both very happy, and I saved more money for her bus fare.

I still worked at the restaurant but had moved to a different shelter, where I volunteered. I kept so busy that I had no time to think about my situation. Eliza arrived on a Saturday. When I went to the bus station to pick her up, I was so nervous. I thought to myself that, after five years, I was going to be able to hug my daughter again. I wondered if I would recognize her. She was ten when I last saw her and now was fifteen. In the distance, I saw a young woman pulling a suitcase, with a large stuffed animal in her hand. I yelled, "Eliza," and she ran toward me. We hugged for a long time and cried. We were oblivious to people passing by. I told her how beautiful she was, and she told me that I looked a little bit older, but just as pretty.

Eliza and I spent a wonderful month together, and we confirmed again that, in addition to being mother and daughter, we are best friends. When the summer was over, Eliza returned to school in the U.S. The young woman I had met at the shelter became our friend, and she accompanied Eliza during her border crossing and put her on the bus home. The goodbye was difficult and sad. By that time, I was living with the older lady I met the first day I arrived in Tijuana. After saying goodbye to my daughter, I was very sad. My heart broke that day. I cried until I couldn't cry anymore. I felt I was missing a part of me and I could not keep going. I immediately made plans to cross the U.S.-Mexico border. I needed my daughter.

Four friends were going to cross the border with me. We planned everything as best we could and thought that everything was going to go well. That was not the case.

We left at 4:00 a.m. The guide was drunk and high, and we got lost. I almost died. I fell into quicksand that almost devoured me. My friends threw a thick stick toward me and pulled me out. I emerged completely naked—the quicksand had consumed my clothes. I looked like a green and black monster. My feet were twisted, and I had a very difficult time walking. Everyone tried to help me. The border patrol spotted us, and we were detained.

I waited for an ambulance at the immigration station. Everyone who saw me seemed horrified. When I left the hospital, they brought me to where I am now. I am imprisoned again and face forty-eight months of prison because I tried to cross the border illegally, with an aggravated felony on my record.

My lawyer seems like a good person, and I trust him. But this place is worse than any of the others where I have been. I want this to end soon. Eliza knows that I am here. I am embarrassed to write her, but I have to. I need her letters to feed my heart.

This prison separates me from my daughter. I tried to cross the border because I wanted to be with her, but I was detained by the border patrol and again I find myself in a cell. Again, I am simply a number. I will be sentenced in December. I had planned to spend Christmas with my daughter. Instead I will probably spend it behind bars.

Melvin Wright

Silent Tears

H ave you ever been lost in a place you're very familiar with? Or been alone in a crowded room? Have you ever been so anxious to get somewhere, yet so afraid to arrive? If you've ever been incarcerated for a significant period of time, you can probably relate to these questions. I can definitely relate.

Let me tell you a story that may give you some insight into the fear, the loneliness, and the feeling of being lost and out of place. Allow me to take you on a journey of returning to society after incarceration.

In 1995 I was given a prison sentence of ten years to life for burglary in the third degree. It was mandatory that I get life on the end because I was a three-time loser, with an extensive criminal history dating back to the early seventies. For the record, I'm a fifty-five-year-old black man who just can't seem to kick a drug addiction that's haunted me most of my life. Committing burglaries was a means to support my addiction.

After being arrested in 1994 and sentenced in 1995, I spent twelve years behind bars in the New York State Department of Correctional Services. I was granted parole in 2006. To say that I was happy to learn that I was going home would be an understatement. The joy that I felt upon learning that I was finally going to see the streets of New York again just couldn't be described.

My joy, however, was also bittersweet because, only weeks before, I'd been informed by the facility's imam (and I'm not Muslim) that my mother had passed away. My mom was one of my biggest supporters, not only during my years of incarceration and other trials and tribulations, but also in all of my positive endeavors. To learn she had died was a devastating blow. What made it especially hard was that it was unexpected. She died of cancer, and I never even knew she was sick. I hadn't seen her for almost eight years. According to family members, she made everyone promise not to tell me because she didn't want me to worry.

I had initially planned to live with my mother if I was granted parole because my girlfriend had moved back with her parents after I was sent upstate. I also knew that my other family members really didn't want me living with them. I could not blame them, considering my track record. However, after my mother's passing, I had to hurry and come up with a suitable address if I wanted to have a chance of making parole. So I begged, pleaded, and cajoled one of my sisters to allow me to be paroled to her address until I could get on my feet. She finally agreed.

On July 7, 2006, I was released from Watertown Correctional Facility and given forty dollars and a bus ticket to New York City. I was told to report to the parole office in Brooklyn in the next twenty-four hours. I was finally on my way. I could hardly wait to see my girlfriend of eighteen years, the love of my life! With sex being the first thing on the agenda, I was impatient to get home, and was already forgiving her for not paying me a visit those last two years. After all, she did continue to write me consistently. I could hardly wait to hold her in my arms and make love to her again.

Yes, I was ecstatic to be taking that five- to six-hour bus ride. But somewhere along the way my joy and happiness slowly turned into fear and apprehension. I can't say what brought about this change, but as I looked at the people sitting on the bus I started to feel as though I didn't belong.

I started to think about what was ahead of me, and what I was gonna do to survive. I had forty dollars in my pocket, my parole release papers with a bunch of rules stipulating what I must do to remain free, and a prison ID card. I started wondering what my girlfriend's situation was like. As I said, it had been about two years since I had last seen her.

I arrived in New York at the Port Authority Bus Terminal around 2:00 p.m. The number of people I saw running around stunned me. I couldn't remember it ever being that crowded. The first thing I did was seek out a phone so that I could call my girlfriend and let her know I was on my way to her mom's house. But as weird as it may sound, I couldn't find one that worked. Being anxious and in a hurry, I really didn't try too hard. I just figured I would surprise her when I got there.

On the subway ride, I thought not only about how my girl hadn't come to visit me, but also about how she hadn't even shown up for my mom's wake and funeral. I found myself getting angry. She and my mother had a very close relationship, and I really couldn't understand how she could have been so indifferent like that. Shortly after my mom's funeral, I'd written my girl a letter cursing her out and accusing her of seeing another man.

By the time I arrived at my subway stop in Manhattan and was walking to her mom's house, I'd made up my mind that I was going to confront her about that issue. When I knocked on her mom's door, I was ready to let her have it verbally. Her mom answered the door, and when she showed me such a tremendous amount of love, I calmed down considerably. After she finished telling me how happy she was to see me home, she told me my girl, Naomi, was in her room. She wasn't doing too well, her mom said, and would be happy to see me. She told me to go right in.

Well, when I walked into my girl's room I got the surprise of my life! To my shock and dismay, she was lying in her bed propped up on several pillows, surrounded by all kinds of medication vials. She was nothing but skin and bones.

"Naomi, what's going on?" I asked her.

She started crying and refused to look at me. At that moment my heart was really hurting for her, so I started hugging and kissing her and telling her how much I loved her. After she calmed down, I asked what was wrong, and she told me she had been sick for a little over two years, which was why she hadn't been coming to see me. The doctors had told her she had ovarian cancer, but that they had gotten it all. I couldn't believe what I was hearing, knowing my mother had just recently died of cancer. I told her not to worry, that I was there now and was going to be there for her through thick and thin.

Right about then I noticed Naomi's mother standing at the bedroom door, motioning for me to come talk to her. So I told my girlfriend I'd be right back, and that when I returned, she had better be ready to pucker up because I wanted to taste some of those sweet kisses of hers that I'd been missing. That got a big smile out of her, like I knew it would.

I found her mother in the kitchen drinking coffee and looking out the window with pain written all over her face. Without looking at me, she told me that she should have warned me first, but she wanted me to see for myself before she gave me the bad news. She told me that there was nothing more that could be done, that she didn't know why Naomi told me that the doctors had gotten it all. She said that it was just a matter of time, and that all they could do was try to make her as comfortable as possible. Naomi had refused to be admitted to the hospital because she didn't want to miss my phone call once a month. Once again, I was shocked by what I was hearing. Right away the feeling of guilt swarmed over me. Something I feel to this very day.

After talking with her mom for a few minutes, I really wanted to spend as much time with Naomi as I possibly could before I left to go to my sister's house in Brooklyn. As soon as I got back to her room, I asked her if she was going to be stingy with the kisses. She leaned toward me, and I hugged her real tight. She moaned in pain, so I let her go. She said she was sorry but it hurt in her bones. Hearing her say she was sorry brought tears to my eyes. I told her it was okay, that all we needed was our lips anyway, and once again she smiled. So I kissed her and shoved my tongue in her mouth so she wouldn't think I found her undesirable, even though I knew that sex between us was out of the question. As I sat there tenderly holding and caressing my girl, I realized that all that time I was thinking negative thoughts about her, writing letters accusing her of cheating on me, and using harsh and threatening words on the phone with her, she was out here fighting a losing battle for her life.

So I asked her why she hadn't told me what was going on. And believe it or not, her response to me was, "I didn't want you in that place worrying about me." My guilt just got heavier and heavier. I couldn't believe this was happening. My girl didn't smoke; she didn't drink or get high on any kind of illegal drugs. She never actually saw me high on drugs, but she'd been told by my mom that I had a drug problem. She told me once that I'd better not be out there putting something in my body that could kill me and leave her all alone in the world. I couldn't even smoke cigarettes in her presence without her becoming angry about it.

I knew I had to get to Brooklyn, so I told my girl that I would be by to see her after I reported to my parole officer the next day. Before I left, I called my sister and told her I was on my way. The first thing she said to me was, "Don't bring anybody home with you because I don't like people coming to my house." I told her, "No problem. I'll be there in a little while." When I got there, she gave me a key and ran down her house rules. Then she went to her bedroom and closed the door. In the living room was an air mattress already inflated with sheets, blanket, and pillows, so I knew this was where I would sleep. Without bothering to eat, I settled in to watch a little TV. I must have dozed off because the next thing I knew it was morning and I had to get up and go report to my parole officer.

When I arrived, I found a long line of other parolees waiting to sign in. About three hours later, I finally heard my name called by a relatively young, slightly overweight black woman. I soon learned that things were slowly going from bad to worse, because she immediately started talking down to me. I wasn't in her office ten minutes before she started threatening me with prison if I failed to do this or failed to do that. By the time I left her office I was convinced that the woman held some kind of deep-seated hatred of men in general.

As the days went by and I got on my grind trying to get a job, traveling here and there on the subway, my funds started to get low and I realized that things were gonna get a lot rougher before they got better. I decided to call my other sister; she lived in New Rochelle with her husband and son. My sister's husband, whom I have always been cool with, answered the phone. He told me he had planned to call me because he had a job lined up for me paying $15 an hour. He said I needed to come out to New Rochelle that Tuesday so that he could go over things with me. I told him I would have to clear it with my parole officer first because Tuesday was my report day. He said, "Fine," but it had to be Tuesday because that was going to be the only day he would be at that office. I told him I was strapped for money and couldn't use public transportation. He said, "Don't worry. I got you. I'll hit you with something when you come out to New Rochelle on Tuesday."

After we hung up I called my parole officer and told her that I would be coming in late because I had a job interview in New Rochelle. Her response was that I would be at her office bright and early Tuesday morning or I would find myself back behind bars Tuesday night. Then she hung up on me. I was pissed off, but I didn't want to get on her bad side any more than I already was. Besides, I didn't think she had a good side.

By this time I'd been home a little over two weeks, pounding the pavement, filling out job applications everywhere. I'd been spending as much time with Naomi as I was able to squeeze in between searching for a job and having to be in the house by my 9:00 p.m. curfew. I tried to get my P.O. to let me spend a weekend with Naomi in light of her condition, but she in no uncertain terms told me, "When hell freezes over." I still hadn't had sex yet, but that wasn't about to happen with Naomi and me anyway. I just wanted to be there for her the way she was there for me all those years.

My P.O. knew of my girlfriend's condition from my sister. Somewhere along the way, she and my sister had become bosom buddies. Knowing my sister, I didn't see that as a good thing. That Tuesday I reported to my P.O.'s office and was immediately called in. I had a bad feeling she was once again going to satisfy one of her sadistic urges. At first she had me fooled because she started out asking me about my girlfriend and how she was doing, and about what I'd been up to that week. I told her my girlfriend wasn't doing too well. I also gave her my update—I'd gone to the D.M.V. and got a state ID; I'd dropped applications for employment in quite a few places; I had applied for public assistance. She told me that was good because my sister had some concerns about the grocery bill that I was accumulating. I told her that was news to me because my sister hadn't mentioned anything to me.

"Well, she mentioned it to me," she said. "As a matter of fact, she called me right after you left the house to come here this morning."

"Why?" I asked. "Why would she call you knowing I'm on my way here?"

"Because I asked her to call me," she said. "And what's this about your going to Westchester County on some cockamamie job interview?"

Before I could respond, she went on to tell me that if she even heard of me going into Westchester County she would have me behind bars so fast my head would spin. And, if I didn't believe her, try her. I was confused at this point, so I asked her why I couldn't go into Westchester County. Isn't it a part of New York State?

She said, "For you, it's out of bounds. You're not to go anywhere outside of the five boroughs."

I just couldn't leave well enough alone, so I asked her, "Why is it out of bounds?"

"Because I say it is, and that's all that matters," she told me.

I was so disappointed because I really wanted that job. Just then, the phone on her desk rang. After picking it up and listening a minute, she said, "He's sitting right here in front of me."

After a few more seconds passed I heard her say, "Okay, I'll tell him right now." She hung up the phone, looked at me and said, "That was your sister on the phone, and she wanted me to tell you that your girlfriend's mother called to let you know that Naomi passed away this morning. She needs you to come to her house as soon as you can."

When I heard this, all I could do at that moment was take a deep breath and hang my head. My P.O. told me to go do what I needed to do, but to be sure to keep her posted. She then asked if I was all right. I told her I felt like everything was coming down on me too fast, that things were stressing me out.

Her response was, "Look, I'm not your therapist, okay? I'm your parole officer and I'm here to lock you up the minute you fuck up." Those were her exact words, and they stung me so bad that tears just came to my eyes before I could compose myself. I got up and left so she wouldn't notice; I was too embarrassed to let her see me crying. After I left her office, I had to decide if I was going to walk from Brooklyn to Manhattan, where Naomi's mother lived, or take the train there and walk back to my sister's house. I only had one more fare on my MetroCard so I knew I'd have to walk either going or coming. Since the walk was shorter coming back to my sister's house, I decided to take the train there and walk back. Besides, Naomi's mom was waiting for me.

When I got there, I expected to find a house filled with friends and relatives; Naomi had plenty of cousins, aunts, and uncles on both sides of her family. But to my surprise and consternation, the only person there was Naomi's mom. She told me she didn't have the strength to deal with things at that time. She needed me to make arrangements to have Naomi's body picked up, as well as get in touch with other family members. I didn't know what to do, but before I could say anything, she went in her bedroom and closed the door. She left me standing there the same way my sister had done.

I grabbed her address book, called one of Naomi's aunts and explained the situation to her. She politely apologized for Naomi's mom putting me in that situation, and said she would get dressed and come right over. I kindly told her that I didn't mind taking care of things, but I just didn't know what to do, or whom I was supposed to call. She said it was okay, that Naomi's mom was probably still in shock, even though they were all expecting this. I understood that, because even though I was expecting my girl to die, I found it hard to believe she was gone. Just to think that two weeks earlier, she had taught me how to use a cell phone so that I could call her during the day when I wasn't there with her. I remembered how she thought it was so funny that I didn't know you had to push the "send" button before your call would go out.

While waiting for Naomi's aunt, I went in the room and sat with her body. I cried silent tears as I thought about all the years we spent together, all the good times, and the rough times. The petty arguments we had and the make-up sex. I even found myself laughing at some of the funny memories.

Just as I thought I might be actually losing my mind sitting there next to my girlfriend's dead body, laughing, the doorbell rang. It was Naomi's aunt. By the time I let her in, Naomi's mother had come out of her room to see who was at the door. As soon as she saw her sister, she broke down crying. While her sister consoled her, she turned to me, grabbed my hand, and said, "You're all I have now. Naomi loved you so much and you need to know that." I did know that, more so then than at any other time in my life. Her aunt told me that I could leave, that she would take care of things and call and let me know what arrangements had been made. So I went back to Brooklyn, walking all the way with a very heavy heart, and a mind full of guilt. The following week passed in a sort of fog. Not even my parole officer's attitude had any effect on me.

Finally, the day of Naomi's funeral rolled around, and I wanted to get there early so that I could spend some time with some of her relatives whom I hadn't seen in awhile. It was then that I learned her mother had requested that she be buried in the family plot in New Jersey. This presented a problem, because New Jersey was another state and was definitely out of bounds for me. I decided to call my P.O. on her cell phone, since it was the weekend and her office was closed. I got her voice mail. I left a message telling her the situation and that I would call again after I returned from the cemetery. I did exactly that as soon as we arrived back in Manhattan. Once again I got her voice mail. I left another message along with my cell phone number. I felt sure that everything would be all right since I'd kept her informed of my every move. Surely she would understand, considering the circumstances. Boy, how wrong I was!

That Tuesday I arrived at my P.O.'s office bright and early. I was one of the first people called. As soon as I walked into her office, a male P.O. standing there told me to turn around and place my hands behind my back. He then put handcuffs on me and proceeded to search me thoroughly.

After he finished searching me, my parole officer looked at me and said, "You think you can just do what you want to do, don't you? Who gave you permission to leave the state?"

I told her that I had called her cell phone and left messages letting her know my every move. I said that I only wanted to bury my girl—nothing else. She told me she didn't care if I wanted to bury the president of the United States, and that if she didn't say it was okay for me to breathe I'd better drop dead right on the spot. As soon as she said this, I noticed her partner, who was also a woman, and the male P.O. who handcuffed me look at each other like they couldn't believe their own ears.

Around this time the supervising parole officer walked in. She told me to take a seat and tell her what I felt she should know about this situation. I told her that when my girlfriend died, my P.O. was the one who gave me the news and told me to go handle my business, but just to keep her informed. I explained how I'd found out at the last minute that my girlfriend was going to be buried in New Jersey, and that I would have felt embarrassed and humiliated if I had to tell her mother that I couldn't attend the burial. I told the supervising parole officer about all the calls I'd made to my P.O. to inform her of every step I made. She asked my P.O. whether I had indeed called her several times, and she said that I had.

In the end, my P.O.'s supervisor told her that maybe she should consider giving me another chance, but to first test my urine and make sure I hadn't gotten high. Well, my urine was clean. So after taking me through another one of her sessions, my P.O. told me that I had gotten off lucky this time, that this one was on her, but that the next one would be on me.

I walked out of her office and started crying. The tears just kept coming. I felt so empty, so all alone, and so afraid. I knew of only one way to get rid of those feelings. I went to where I felt most comfortable, to be with those I felt most comfortable with. I started using again.

Now I'm back where I most hate being, where I'm most uncomfortable, and most afraid. A place where nothing my parole officer could say or do could compare to the misery I must now endure.

Tariq Mayo

The Look on His Face

H e saunters into the mess hall like he owns the place.
Stupid isn't the right word, but it's the first one that
comes to mind. Stupid Ass Jumbo. You should've seen the
look on his face.

His real name—or government name, as we say—is Ramel,
but he's a huge black mass of a man, so everyone calls him
Jumbo.

Jumbo couldn't even stay home for ninety days. Sigh.

I shake my head in the name of recidivism.

And then I shake it some more for all the wasted
opportunities.

Finally, I shake my head because I'm just happy to see
him—but not really happy, if you know what I mean.

His state greens still have those hard state creases in them; they're all shiny and spinach green, with that omnipresent 09 number glowing on his jacket like an avatar.

"I caught a new one," he lip syncs to me, as he falls in line for his steaming scoop of turkey chow mein.

I lip sync back, "A new one?" I display the surprised facial expressions to match. But I'm not really surprised.

See, here's a dude who told me one night in our cube, "The system is designed for us to fail." He went on: "They place guns and drugs in our community, then arrest us for having them. Then once we do finally realize the errors of our ways, it's too late. Our records are too messed up to get any type of substantial employment, and it's back to the streets to feed our families. The vicious cycle continues." He looked down at me from the top bunk and said, "From the womb to the tomb."

All I could think to say at that time was, "Man, I got twenty-eight months left."

After wolfing down my generic Oriental treat, I slow drag for Jumbo on the walkway. I need details, I tell myself.

He just left here eighty-five days ago. Eighty-five days? That's 2,040 hours. Go 'head, do the math. I'll wait. That's eleven state movies. That's six commissary buys. In fact, it's still the same season it was when he left. I still have deodorant I bought when he was here.

What would make a person want to come back here? What is so important that he would give up his freedom in return for this locked-down lifestyle, this "gated community?" Again, stupid isn't the best word, but it's the first one that comes to mind.

Okay, so maybe this isn't my fifth bid—and no, I don't have a prison number that signifies I've been locked up since the nineties. But once I'm released, I can't even imagine doing anything even remotely criminal. Selling drugs; yeah, right. You'd have to drag me across the street kicking and screaming to even get me to go when the sign says DON'T WALK. A first-class ticket to the Playboy Mansion couldn't pull me away from making my parole appointment. I mean, if someone slapped my mama, I'd be like, "HEY...what'd she do?" Maybe I'm exaggerating a little bit, but you see where I'm going.

So Jumbo finally catches up with me on the walkway.

He says, "It was my baby moms, man. I got into it with her boyfriend, the one she said she wasn't dealing with anymore. He put his hands on her and one thing led to another, and...I stabbed him."

"You stabbed him?" I say, with more surprised facial expressions. They're so helpful in moments like these.

"Yeah," he says, all excited like he's reliving the moment in his head. "And guess what this gangsta does, man?"

Having heard dozens of these kinds of stories before, I say, "He calls the cops."

"He calls the PO-LICE, MAN! Can you believe that?"

"I can believe it," I say. "She should've called the police before she called you."

He says, "Yeah, right."

I say, "Yeah, right."

We walk the walkway in silence for a second, then I break the monotony. "So what kinda time you lookin' at?"

"Five years!" he says, adding his own surprised facial expressions. His are way more convincing than mine.

And now I have to squeeze out some artificial sympathy for my troubled friend. "You so stupid, son!" I say. "Ain't nothin' out there worth your freedom, man. Not money. Not women. Not nothin', man. And I bet she's still messin' with that same dude!"

He makes a serious face. "Nah, man. She said that's over."

"That's what she said," I say.

Serious face again. "Nah, for real, man."

And I say, "But I bet you still messin' with her."

He gives me a smiley face now. "That's my baby moms, man. You know how that go."

Before we return to our respective dorms, we shake hands and hug. It does feel kinda good to see an old buddy—even under these circumstances.

Then he looks me in the eyes, all serious-like. "What's up with you, though? You alright?"

All I can think to say is, "Man, I got nine months left."

There was no facial expression I could make that could portray my anxiety.

Robert Cepeda

Back on the Block

There's an old saying: "Those that fail to plan, plan to fail." I wish I had heard of that proverb before I was released from prison.

On my last day behind the wall I woke up early, washed up with the cold water in my sink, and got ready to go. Forget breakfast. I was ready to go. I had been away five years. I had spent most of that time playing basketball, lifting weights, or walking around the yard and telling old street tales with my homies. Most of our stories were slight exaggerations and, at times, total fabrications. But, hey, it was a way to pass the time, and time was all we had. That morning all I could think was that it was finally over. I paced back and forth waiting for my cell door to open. I was ready to go.

On the long bus ride home, I took in every sight as if I had just arrived in America from some distant land. My sentence was two-and-a-half to five years. I could have been released at my minimum sentence if I had participated in the educational, vocational, and transitional programs offered. But I had decided I didn't need that bookworm stuff, so I was forced to do the maximum.

I arrived at the Port Authority bus terminal in Manhattan and headed to the subway. Almost immediately, a girl who looked no more than seventeen approached me. She had spotted my jailhouse net bag filled with a few precious belongings like family photos and letters. Knowing I had just come home, she asked if I wanted to have sex for twenty bucks.

As tempting as it sounded—and she wasn't half bad looking—spending half of my complimentary forty dollars release money on some strange girl who may be jailbait and have AIDS was not worth the risk. I politely declined and caught the train to the Bronx.

I had no game plan. I didn't think I needed one. I had family to go home to—my mother's house. I had friends who would be glad to see me and hit me with some quick cash. And after I visited my ex-girlfriend Vanessa and got some much needed sexual healing, I would worry about finding a job. In truth, Vanessa had stopped writing me a year after my incarceration, but I just knew that after she saw me again those feelings would come flooding back. She would fling herself into my arms and beg my forgiveness. At least that's how I imagined it while I was in prison.

The funny thing about life is that it catches up with you while you're daydreaming. My mom didn't tell me that her brother, Uncle James, had lost his job six months earlier, couldn't make the rent, and lost his apartment. He had moved into my old room. Mom assured me I would be comfortable on the couch until I got a job and made enough to get my own place.

Those friends of mine weren't doing anything. Five years, and they were still right on the same corner where I had left them. At least Angel and Willie were. Clayton was dead—shot in the back while stealing drugs. Darryl was on Rikers Island, about to go upstate. The other members of my old crew were scattered in the wind.

Vanessa? She had two kids—a four-year-old and a two-year-old—by the neighborhood drug dealer, Prince. No wonder she stopped writing. They pulled up in a Ford Explorer. She said, "Hi," when she saw me, and walked her snotty-nosed brats into her apartment building. Her man, Prince, asked if I wanted to sell some crack to "get on my feet." I said, "No."

The next few weeks I looked for a job. There were none available for an ex-offender that would have paid enough to rent an apartment. The jobs were mostly street sweepers, food delivery, and backbreaking labor jobs. But I couldn't even get hired for some of these because I had no G.E.D. or vocational skills. I used to laugh at those nerds in prison who only wanted to watch the news on TV and read about the economy in *Time* or *BusinessWeek*. Even in prison I guess it's good to know what trends are out there, especially if you plan on being released one day.

Eventually, my mom's couch got to be too much. I was wearing old clothes from five years ago and didn't have many options. I went to see Prince for some work. Angel and Willie both said it was a bad idea, but they weren't doing nothing but holding up the corner pole. I started with a few ounces of crack.

Lots of things change in five years, including police personnel and their surveillance. I was caught with two ounces of crack cocaine and sent back to jail. On Rikers Island, I saw my friend Darryl. I would be going upstate right behind him.

This time around I'm reading newspapers whenever I can. There's a recession out there. They say the economy's on the rebound, but I think it's a good idea to keep an eye on things and come up with a good plan for my next release.

Tamara Anderson

Entering the Lotus Seed

It was early in my stay at the Lotus Seed Zen Center, on one of the social evenings that Samson called "pasta and a movie" night. He claimed that these events were an option for people who had nowhere else to go—people who no longer partied, people who had lost much in their lives. I suspected that they were also about staving off his own loneliness. And Kurt's. I gathered that they had spent many Friday and Saturday nights together, two forgotten old men full of war stories, heating up frozen pizza and watching lurid action movies. That night Samson seemed at ease, happy to be surrounded by people.

Kurt, Jill, and Mary Anne were there. But I wished that everyone would go home. The girls irked me. Jill, an overbearing, privileged pain in the ass, kept asking me questions about myself that I couldn't answer. Mary Anne—tall, blonde, slim Mary Anne—a nice person really, if I could see past her youth and perfection. According to Samson, she'd had quite a brush with drugs. I was jealous; they were young and pretty and had everything to be hopeful for, and there I was, not a young woman anymore, and I had squandered all of my opportunities in life. I felt stuck in life and stuck in the state of Florida, a mindset all its own.

I wanted to move the evening along, so I cleared some dishes from the table and went through the swinging doors to the kitchen.

I carefully stacked dishes beside the sink. Then, at the low cupboard in the corner of the kitchen, I reached behind a large rice cooker for a coffee mug I'd already filled with white wine, and took a drink. The bottle was stashed there, too. I was not supposed to be drinking, but I didn't have a great track record of following rules.

As each of the girls left, I watched the way Samson hugged them. Jill, who wasn't wearing a bra, seemed to rub up against him in a suggestive way. Mary Anne, on the other hand, hugged him like a daughter. Samson had a sort of glazed expression. I wondered what was going through his mind.

Kurt was the last to leave, to make his shift as a night security guard. He was an old friend of Samson's from his days as a Tibetan Buddhist. But unlike Samson, with his Army major's pension and medical benefits, Kurt had to work a low-paying job, despite his poor health.

"Stay out of trouble, young man!" called Samson.

Later, Samson stood in front of the kitchen sink washing dishes as I put away the leftovers and cleaned the counters.

Suddenly he held up his soapy hands and looked at them.

"What's wrong?" I asked.

"Getting old sucks," he said, putting his hands back in the dishwater. "You know, kiddo, washing dishes always reminds me of the time early in my military career when I screwed up and got thirty days of mess duty. At the end of the thirty days, I smart-mouthed my sergeant and got thirty more. That's what motivated me to get so much rank so fast. I still hate washing dishes."

He had told me before about his four years as a Marine in Vietnam, and then his time in Special Forces in Central America. After a friend was assassinated in El Salvador, he somehow found his way to Buddhism.

"Well, I'm done," I said. "Are you done?"

"Yes," he said, placing a last bowl in the full drain board.

"Okay, I feel like watching TV. Is there something you want to watch?"

The round oak table that served for dining was still in the middle of the room, so we moved it to the corner where it stayed when there were no guests. It was an odd living arrangement; the house was a spiritual center of sorts that served many functions: it was Samson's home; it was the Zen center of which he was the teacher, and it was an acupuncturist's office. The room where we ate and watched TV was also the room where I folded out the futon couch every night and slept.

We had gotten into the habit of watching TV each night before bed. Samson sat at one end of the couch and I curled up at the other. We watched vapid crime shows which, just then, I didn't mind.

Samson did not last long in front of the television that night.

"Kiddo, it's time for me to hit the fart-sack," he said.

"Nice language," I said. "How come you're so tired? I did all the cooking."

"You got me. All I know is I've got about enough battery power left to get the cats in and then die."

"Are you okay?"

"I'm fine, just tired. I have all that driving to prison tomorrow." He stood up. "Good night, kiddo." And he saluted me from the doorway.

"Okay, good night."

I made up the futon then went to the kitchen and poured some wine. I stood in the dark and looked through the kitchen window into night, without really seeing anything. This strangeness would strike me at any moment of the day since I'd gotten out of jail, and I would find myself squinting at nothing, at some vanishing point. How I had ended up here, in this place, at this time, with these people, seemed profound and barely believable. But then I would look back through my life and see the inevitable trajectory that only I could know, that had led me to this point, as if by grand design.

I quietly unlocked the front door and sat on the porch step. The porch was littered with leaves and stray Spanish moss that I would sweep in the morning. I did as much as I could around the house; at the moment, it was all I had to offer in exchange for the help I was receiving. I had never in my life accepted something for nothing, never allowed an imbalance in giving and receiving to stand long between myself and anyone else. I reminded myself that this place was all I had, both a shock and a comfort. Either way, I had no right to fuck it up. In the backyard I flung the last of the wine into the fern patch and went inside.

In the morning at 6:30 sharp, Samson and I and a few others met in the Dharma Room for a half hour of sitting. At the end we chanted the Four Great Vows: Sentient beings are numberless. We vow to save them all. Delusions are endless. We vow to cut through them all. The teachings are infinite. We vow to learn them all. The Buddha way is inconceivable. We vow to attain it.

After meditation, Samson went on his ritual morning bike ride across the university campus to the bagel shop where, as he said, he'd been exchanging lies with the same group of retirees for years.

For a time after each meditation session, I felt still and blank and not unhappy. As if I were in a state of grace, unsullied, new. In jail, where there was nothing to do, and nothing expected, I felt insulated from normal daily responsibilities and concerns. This feeling increased as I tried to meditate. By one act, everything had been taken from me, or I had let everything go—in no time I had gone from being a graduate student in English to nothing. But now I was somewhere in between. And with every day that passed, the newness waned, choices presented themselves, and old patterns, paths in my mind, opened.

I was sweeping the front porch when Samson got home from his bike ride.

"Full of energy this morning, I see!" he said.

"Yes, I suppose so."

"So good to come home to a human being! You don't know how many times I've come home to no one but the cats."

"I made you some lunch to take on your drive," I said.

"Not going on a drive today," he said, mopping sweat from his forehead with the blue kerchief.

"No? How come?" I asked. This was unlike him—he never canceled prison visits.

"Tired, kiddo; didn't sleep so well."

"Hmmm, well maybe you need to take a nap then."

"A nap! I'm not back in diapers yet, kid," he said.

"Do you think you're sick? Want me to get you something?"

"Not sure, but maybe a little rest is a good idea," he said before going inside.

Later that afternoon, after Samson had rested, we sat in his little home office, me on one computer and Samson on another. He was working on an editorial for the local paper about the recidivism problem and the lack of programs to help former inmates make a successful transition. I was acting as editor. His writing style drove me crazy—he developed it as a Cold War propagandist, and I kept pointing out the breaks in his logic, his hyperbole.

"Don't you think it's hot in here?" I said. Then I went to the center of the room and pulled the chain of the ceiling fan. I felt my shirt lift as I stretched, and Samson's eyes on me.

"Don't lose that," he said. "I know some women who would kill to have your body."

"I'm not on display here, you know," I said.

"It's a compliment. I know some women who would kill for that, too." He changed the subject. "So, kiddo, let's talk about your plans."

"What plans?"

"If I had the money, I'd give you a job myself, but…"

"I don't expect you to give me a job," I said. "I just don't know where or how to look. There aren't a lot of options for me in this stupid little town, you know, even if I weren't a criminal."

"I know. That's why I'm going to contact a friend of mine, a very nice lady who runs a copy shop over by the mall. She hired a guy I worked with out of prison about five years ago, best employee she ever had, but his liver gave out. Hep C. Whenever I see her, she tells me to send more people her way."

"A copy shop?"

"It beats McDonald's."

"This is true. And I do have the State of Florida breathing down my neck to get a job, or else. But don't you think this is a little too much?"

"What do you mean?"

"I mean you're doing so much for me. You've given me a place to live, you feed me, you take me places, you gave me a bike, and now you're getting me a job? Do you do this much for everyone?"

"No, not for everyone," he said, "but when I see something special, I like to do a little extra. I fully expect that within a year, you'll be making a good living doing what you do best.

Consider this job a stepping stone. You're smart and you've got a lot of talents. You've got work to do, no question, but I'm a hundred percent sure you're gonna make it."

"You think so, huh?"

"Yes, ma'am, I do. Now, why don't we have some of that leftover ice cream?"

"Ice cream? Wow, this is the treatment!"

"We operate a full-service organization here."

"So I see," I said.

It was nearly a month since I'd been released, and the prospect of a job was frightening to me because I did not know who I was anymore and it seemed I would have to be a person who was convicted of a crime, who must always plead for a break, prove myself over and over. I had already done so much of this, struggling up from the random, violent, squalid life my family had brought me into, struggling to get my head above water, to a place where I could breathe.

Later that night, after watching television, Samson hugged me good night.

"Touch is important, kiddo. You know?" he said.

"I know," I said.

The hugs became a ritual after that—in the morning after meditation and at night before bed. A good-morning hug and a good-night hug.

The following week, Samson took me to the copy shop. As he had predicted, I hit it off with Susan, the owner. She asked me to start the next day.

"I feel good about this," I said, as Samson drove us home.

"Really good. Thank you." I felt overwhelming gratitude toward Samson—without him, I had nowhere to go, and nothing. I felt like kissing him, so I leaned over and did.

Before bed that night, in the dark kitchen, we hugged for a long time.

I recalled the moment when I noticed Samson. It was in jail when I was being escorted by a guard to the visiting cell to see him. Sex was the furthest thing from my mind then. But when I saw him there, leaning in the doorway at the end of the hall rather than sitting in the cell on his side of the grill, I became aware of him as a man. He was tall, broad-shouldered—a strong man still. He wore a black-collared short-sleeved shirt and slacks. His belt was riding midway under a gut that he carried well. He looked amused, commanding, and comfortable all at once. During those visits he usually had to leave first, and always with an apology. As I'd wait for a guard to take me back, I'd hear him whistling down those halls where no one whistled. Whistling in the dark.

The next morning, with me dressed in a flowered skirt for my first day of work, Samson took me onto his lap and kissed me.

After that, we fell into the routine of secrecy. This was not at all what I had expected of Zen center living. Samson had warned me several times, both during his visits in jail and early in my stay with him: I'm not your father, your boyfriend, or your therapist. And the advice: Wait at least a year before getting into any romantic relationship. But how could I, a person who never expected or imagined my life could be so disastrously altered, that I could be brought so low, question this? It fit somehow, being with Samson, despite our age difference of nearly thirty years.

It was a few weeks into the affair, on a Saturday, when Samson had the heart attack. I drove him to the emergency room. On the way, while Samson struggled to breathe between waves of pain, he kept telling me not to ride the clutch of his truck.

"I think you should focus on breathing," I said, and gripped the steering wheel harder than anything I ever gripped in my life.

Ninety percent blockage in two arteries; sixty percent in two others.

When I visited Samson the day before his surgery, we joked and laughed over a useless game of Scrabble. Then Kurt showed up; he and Samson volleyed insults.

"I'd say ya looked good if it would make any difference," Kurt said.

"You'll be on this side of the bed pan soon enough, young man."

"Since the get well cards are for people who at least got a fifty-fifty chance, I got you this sympathy card instead."

"You know what sympathy is?" Samson asked. "It's a word in the dictionary between shit and syphilis."

Then Samson got up to pee, his hospital robe not quite covering his backside; we broke into giggles. As we prepared to leave, Samson kissed me on the mouth, in front of Kurt. "You're good medicine, kiddo."

The next day, I went to the hospital after work. The first thing I noticed when I entered Samson's room was how shrunken he looked, crumpled to one side of the bed, his head hidden by a pillow. I stood close and listened to him breathe. The petals of the supermarket chrysanthemums I'd brought the day before littered the floor. As I moved around his bed to straighten things, my shoes stuck. A container half full of urine was hooked askew onto the rail of his bed.

Samson stirred then and inched over onto his back.

"Kiddo, is that you?"

"Yes," I said, seeing the redness of his face and neck.

"Hand me my glasses."

I did.

"Sit down."

I sat at the end of the bed, feeling uncertain and nervous. They'd put four stents into his heart, jamming them up the large artery in his groin.

"I could cry," he said.

"I could cry, too," I said. I moved from the end of the bed to his side, where I buried my face in his unwashed neck and began to cry.

I cried because the room smelled like urine and because of the unlikely place I found myself. I cried because Samson might die and because he was not at all the man I needed. It was as if we had been following a script, he and I, a pattern of relationships that we had each been repeating for lifetimes. I cried for my ruined life. I cried because all the effort I'd made to leave squalor behind was for nothing. The squalor was deep inside me. I cried because the Buddha was right: life is suffering, old age, sickness and death, inevitable. And how do we get out of this cycle of samsara?

"Please, kiddo, please," Samson said, and had been saying for several minutes. A nurse appeared at the door.

"Okay, okay." Then I climbed out of the bed and looked around the room for something to clean up the spilled urine and dead flower petals.

Delores Mariano

Leaving the Walls Behind

I am ready for someone to push my wheelchair through the gate. I am ready for someone to help me out of hell.

I have my bag of medications, but they forgot my pain medications. Now we must wait in the ninety-degree heat for it to be brought from the pharmacy. Please, I pray, hurry; my oxygen is getting low. I know there is a ride on the other side; I just need to get there. Oh, here comes the officer with the pain medicine—and here I go.

Yes, my ride is waiting, and I get to be pushed down the "out of bounds" road to the van. The air on this side seems so much fresher. The trees—yes, trees—that we don't have behind the walls are still alive and well. Flowers! Oh, and a hug that I can have from my friend who's picking me up that is not limited to five seconds, like in the visiting room. I am free, free, FREE! It hits me with a jolt of reality; I am not behind the walls, not stuck in a twelve-by-eight hospital room anymore. This is life, this is reality, and this is the real world.

I get in the van. I have real money in an envelope in my pocket and get to eat real, recognizable food—not food that you have to guess at. I order a hamburger and onion rings and a shake, and it is what it says it is!

I cry. I cry as I eat. I cry as I look through a van window that I can put up and down. I cry as it all sinks in—I am not in shackles, my hands and feet are FREE! Then I begin to laugh and thank my friend and thank God that I am out of hell and am free. Emotionally, I am in trauma, but I know I will soon land on my two feet in reality.

I see a clothing store, and I am going to shed what remains of hell and buy myself a brand new outfit from the inside out. WOW! The prices are something I did not count on, but I need clothes—pants, a top, sandals, and the things that go under. Well, maybe a bra can wait; I don't have enough for all of that. My own shampoo and conditioner and body wash. I will smell so much better, not moldy and dusty, the way I feel right now.

Next stop, the beauty shop next door for a quick cut and a dye job on my gray hair. My family has not seen me for thirty-seven months, and I am not ready for gray hair. I want to look something like, or close to, what I looked like when I left home. I know I am older; there are wrinkles now where there were none. I feel like I am a hundred, but I am half that.

I am still in a wheelchair, but I plan on getting real therapy and walking again. I can and I will get the right medical doctors, and I will live and no longer worry every day about whether I can get the proper medications when I need them. I won't have the nightmares of being left in my hospital room, pushing a button for help and getting no response from a nurse. I won't worry about being taken to the hospital with no vital signs, almost dead, and then revived. I am FREE, I keep telling myself; yes, I have been released.

I lost my home, and I know my mother and son are in a motel. But at least we have a roof over our heads. Yes, at one o'clock in the morning, there are my mother and my son at the door of their room, waiting for me, arms open, crying, full of loving words. I have waited and yearned for so long to hear the sounds of their voices. I am up out of the van, standing with a cane and taking a few steps at a time. We are in each other's arms, loving and promising never to leave home again.

I know that this is the easy part. The rest of my integration into society will take time, but I will do it! I am alive. I promised to be a voice for those women I left behind those sick walls, and I will do it. But first, I must get my medical care going and my Social Security started. I know we will be out of that motel soon.

The very next day, I am in the Social Security office and find out that they owe me money. I applied for it before I left and it was granted, so I am told that I will have a check by the first of the month. I tell myself that I am fortunate, and that I should just rest, and then go make my plans. I tell myself to do one step at a time, not to push myself. I will wait for the check and then look for a home for my mother, son, and me. Now, to the doctor. There is a clinic around the corner from the motel. I have my son to wheel me around now, so we go there the next day. I tell the truth about where I just came from, show my prescriptions, and the doctor gives me refills. I'm told I don't have to pay—everyone gets a free visit and medications one time. I cry again. I feel blessed and free, and somehow in control of my life again after so long.

The law states that after twenty-eight days, you must leave the motel for twenty-four hours before coming back, so that you are not a permanent resident. We pack up and go to another dwelling for one day. I tell my mother that this is not going to happen again.

It is Thursday and I am looking in Sunday's paper for an apartment. There is one that we can afford because now I have my check. I call, and the owner says that he has seven people who have looked at it, but we can go see it if we'd like. He somehow feels that he should rent it to us, with no credit check. He is a pastor and is giving us a chance. So, we move. I cannot do anything physically, but there are people who come and move everything from storage to the apartment.

I see that all of my clothes are either gone or they are too big, and I get depressed. My friend comes over with two bags of clothes, not even knowing, and then another friend from up north comes down with clothes. I have an overflow of clothes. I just don't know what to think.

The hardships of getting around and the very strict parole officer just don't seem so bad. The need for money for food is on my mind. I ask my son to push me to the store, where I buy a lotto scratcher. I tell my son that I have won twenty dollars. He takes the lotto scratcher to the counter and comes back and tells me I did not win twenty dollars. I am getting depressed because I read it wrong when he hands me a fifty-dollar bill. This is truly being free in the real world, where anything can happen, good and bad, and it is good right now.

———◦◦◦———

With the right doctors, therapy, and family, I have gone through the death of my father and my son, the birth of my granddaughter, the ups and downs of my daughter's drug challenges, a stay in a real hospital, the challenge of wanting to give up when I become sick and can't breathe—and through it all, I am FREE. My eyes look around at my home. We are still here after four years. It may not be what most would call great, but it is home, it is mine, and I am FREE. I can go outside when I want, smell the grass, get in a car and go to the doctor, the store, for a ride, to visit someone, to church, and I don't need to have permission, escorts, and chains. I am FREE.

Now, as I sit here, I cry for all the women I left behind who are in hell, not getting proper medical treatment. They are dying daily and should not be. My heart is there, but I am FREE to tell the story of making it out as a disabled elderly woman.

It is not easy here with real bills, walking problems, and the stigma that still hangs over me. But nothing matters to me anymore than to be thankful each day that I wake up in a real bed when I want to and can do my daily errands.

I can function; I can use a cell phone, and I'm learning to use a computer. I see so many people going by who don't realize the freedom they have to move around, to cry and laugh, to drive wherever they want. I see what I have, and I will not do anything to lose all of this again. Freedom is the greatest gift and I cherish it every day.

I look at you through my words and hope you will see me, for I made it; I am FREE. I need you to know how alive I am now and how dead I was. Incarceration is a death sentence for anyone who is ill. Freedom is a chance at life.

Thank you for seeing me.

Anthony Brown

A Whole New World

S addam Hussein was toppled. The Nintendo Wii turned soccer moms into gamers. Soulja Boy became a hip-hop phenom. And the son of a Kenyan broke the color barrier at 1600 Pennsylvania Avenue. My, how times have changed since my incarceration in 2003. While prisoners' lives seemed to be nothing more than a monotonous loop of counts, commissary, chow, and recreation, the free world became as predictable as Kanye West at an awards show. Through Katrina, wars, and recession, "hope" and "change" became more than campaign buzzwords. They were antidotes for the weary.

Surely razor wire and gun towers cannot render that spirit of renewal powerless. Most prisoners will reenter society. Thus, it behooves us to honestly confront our character flaws and strengthen our individual weaknesses. In doing so, we'll not only be better equipped to lead productive lives, we'll become exemplars of redemption.

First of all, I'm no counselor, religious philosopher, twelve-step facilitator, or any other titleholder authorized to dispense advice. What I am is a father, a convict, a writer, and a budding environmentalist—a student of life who welcomingly accepts all extra-credit assignments to keep from failing. In a maximum-security prison, I looked inside the crevice of my soul and assessed the damage that no marijuana, sexual promiscuity, hip-hop, or any other distracting self-medication could assuage. In a maximum-security prison, I put away my childish sense of victimhood and became a man.

The road I traveled to get there was not easy.

If my mother were to walk through this facility, I'd probably do what any other self-respecting gentleman would do under these unfortunate circumstances—discreetly check her out. But in my case, it wouldn't be because of some Oedipal attraction to my parent. The fact is that I have never laid eyes on the woman. What has amazed me about this unconventional fact of my life is that on the rare occasions I've been comfortable enough with other convicts to exchange brief biographies, they've been consistently stunned. These hardcore, menace-to-society types are absolutely unable to fathom not knowing "mommy."

Truthfully, I never realized just how unbalanced I was due to my unorthodox childhood. I was adopted into a working- to middle-class family in Columbus, Georgia. The father was generous. He gave me his name and three near-death experiences.

To negotiate the release of my absolute favorite Cabbage Patch Kid, I was forced to have sex with my hairy-legged older sister. I was ten years old. I'm not sure which of us should be more embarrassed by the revelation. And I shared a bedroom with the fat sister, nine months my junior, until I was old enough to wear Lifestyles. The chances of a normal teenage life further disintegrated when the father, the mother's husband, bailed out right as she was tipping the scales north of a heavyweight boxer. There I was—his namesake, his gender. And a mid-life-crisis stress reliever. The psychological and physical torment I endured during my stay at the anti-Tyler Perry version of the Browns wasn't exactly the best start in life.

Fast forward to my arrival in Atlanta. I was a directionless young man introduced to abject poverty. Before this tailspin in "Black Mecca," I attempted to live with the original Anthony at his bachelor pad in Ohio. He vehemently resisted the last heart-filled plea I'd ever make. As I rode the Greyhound back to Georgia, with Outkast beating up my eardrums, the likelihood of my entering the prison system had been greatly escalated.

As a criminal novice, I was a disaster. I carried crack and loaded handguns in my pockets like harmless loose change, drove unlicensed getaway cars, and bought Rocawear with the re-up money I was supposed to use to replenish my stash. My pimp hand was as weak as my intuition. I totally disregarded my business acumen and the high performance I had displayed in professional settings during irregular stints at lawful employment. My chaotic underworld hokey-pokey would end with my right foot in Sing Sing state prison and my left foot in the Feds, and with me cathartically writing to turn myself around.

Students of abnormal psychology would probably identify my comfort using ski masks and neckties interchangeably as a split personality disorder. They may be right to some degree. Like many prisoners, I could go through the recriminations of the broken adoption system, horrible public schools, racist criminal justice system, and even slavery. But the truth is that we make choices in life. Whether they are poor or positive, our choices come with effects. Obviously, the ones that led to incarceration weren't the best. The good news is that most of us will get another shot. Here are two keys I think are needed whenever we get that shot.

Proper Preparation

Prison is an animal. It can figuratively and literally tear a man apart. The pure scare factor of the beast is enough to drive a wedge between loved ones. Although love can ultimately conquer fear, some people can't bravely disregard the obnoxious growls—they forget about their imprisoned loved ones, leaving them to fend for themselves against this unsympathetic monster.

It is easy to get caught up in resentment over the current situation and impede the healing process that can come with time. We sometimes mentally check out; the abrasiveness and utter despair of life in confinement makes that a seemingly viable option. Whether that mental checkout is incessant gossiping, drugs, overeating, relentless consumption of pornography, or just staring at the wall, that "option" is a disservice to oneself. We need to use the time preparing for a permanent departure from prison—especially since very few prisoners have the luxury of financial security upon release. And, even if they do, money is no substitute for the social skills that so many prisoners lack.

I view prison as an institution for higher learning—minus the Greek sororities and naked beer slides. And I'm not deluding myself for the sake of sanity. Meaningful education can happen anywhere. Beyond the whole crime and punishment aspect, the learning is continuous in prison. You learn how to get over the sadness and disappointments. There's the crash course in navigating the diversity of personalities. Survival is a case study in itself, and that's just the basics. Advanced learning is possible when a concentrated effort is made to acquire useful knowledge.

The key to successful reentry into society is taking advantage of the time to become intimately knowledgeable about yourself, your skills and passion, so that you can ultimately match your strengths with a career.

That is not to say that getting the job you want in your chosen career will be easy. As ex-convicts, we are guaranteed to encounter hurdles and fiery hoops on the path to a triumphant reentry—and the biggest hurdle is employment. Given the economic uncertainty following the global recession and massive loss of jobs, the marketplace has become much more competitive. Proper preparation involves staying informed. And the most vital part of proper preparation involves being realistic.

By taking into account the changing climate in America's job market, I was able to be realistic and center my studies on my strengths—which include sitting on my behind for long hours and being highly opinionated. Writing is the perfect profession for me because I've always had an affinity for words. Another advantage of my career choice is the ability to practice the craft without waiting for a release date. It's so important to get as much practice in your trade as possible. That way you can hit the ground running.

I'm still perfecting my approach to writing and finding my voice. But what's most important is that I am passionate. In addition to one day operating my own publishing company, my goal is to be the author who bridges the gap between urban-lit and mainstream titles. I've noticed that even the most celebrated urban author rarely surpasses the high laurel of being an *Essence* bestseller. No Oprah Book Club, *New York Times* list, *USA Today* list. Paradoxically, I have the advantage of time to think outside the "chicken snack box." Let's not forget that President Obama ate arugula on the South Side of Chicago!

So, I refused to be antagonized into paralysis by the beast called prison. I kicked the big brute in his butt and told it, "Sit down, Boo-Boo. I've got goals to achieve!"

Etiquette for Excellence

Successful reentry is all about your commitment to opening up a fresh file in your life story and being generous with the exclamation points and smiley faces. Achieving excellence and upward mobility in your life story's new file require a certain etiquette. It includes having great communication skills, making others feel comfortable, and being dependable and unafraid to go the extra distance for a cause greater than yourself. Of course, prison life erodes commonplace manners and other social norms—and most prisoners never acquired healthy lessons in acceptable decorum in the first place. But while you may never learn the difference between a steak knife and butter knife, a "thank you" and "good evening" plus a little charm could have an aristocrat eating out of the palm of your hand. Your washed hand, of course.

There's a grave problem within the black community with scholarly kids being accused of "acting white." Sadly, that level of immaturity in response to academic excellence isn't relegated to the schoolyard. I hope that with the rise of the Obama family, that nonsense will go the way of cassette tapes. As ex-cons, we will have to be able to articulate effectively. Don't get me wrong; I'm all for keeping it real. I'm just as much a hip-hop fanatic as any brother. I even wrote a book on the subject. However, the n-word, profanity, and incomprehensible slang often aren't appropriate. There is no greater self-sabotage than the rebuke of education, especially English. An employer needs a little more than "I need a job 'cause my P.O. gonna violate me." That's unacceptable and a travesty of the English language. When my next shot comes, I plan to respond something like this:

Interviewer: "I see you've been convicted of a felony. Why should my company hire you?"

Me: "My awful experience on the wrong side of the law taught me valuable lessons, the most important being the value of integrity. It was a hard lesson. I see your company's brand as a brand of integrity. It has always offered an alternative to irresponsibility by way of employment. I'm here to join the winning team."

The way you express yourself verbally reflects how people will regard you. There's power in words. Conversely, to our detriment, the power of our might disproportionately trumps our intellect.

Contrary to the unwritten rules of prison, every discrepancy doesn't have to result in violence. It amazes me just how insecure some men behind bars are. Every little thing is a violation and disrespect to their manhood. Please! That type of alpha-male ego-tripping will guarantee problems. Of course, life behind bars is a different animal than societal beefs. But some things you just have to leave behind. Like the shanks. Nobody feels comfortable approaching a ticking time bomb.

Whether on the job or in a relationship, there's a chance people on the outside will learn about our time spent in prison. The burden is on us to be approachable. A screwed-up face may be warranted when entering an exercise yard where killers are bench-pressing the equivalent of a Volvo and gangbangers are eyeing you to see what you're repping. But that same expression could send the wrong message at the dinner table of your girlfriend's parents. It wouldn't hurt to smile and introduce yourself by something other than "Killer."

And there always needs to be a go-to guy. Kobe has Lamar Odom. Spike Lee has Denzel and hip-hop has Lil Wayne. Dependability is a skill that's easy to hone. It's priceless. When we are willing to be selfless, the hand that we offer gets clasped by another. The more selfless you are, the more hands interlock yours. You become part of a community. You can never fall again because your hands are being held by those willing to reciprocate the love you showed.

To illustrate the reality of community, we have to look no further than one of my heroes, Jay-Z. When the 2004 Best of Both Worlds Tour imploded in New York City, a disaster could have unfolded. Madison Square Garden was filled to capacity, but one half of the headline had defected under a cloud of hostility and pepper spray. With R. Kelly gone, Jay could've panicked or refunded tickets. But since he had so much love from the industry because of being a genuine person (for example, the love he showed Pimp C while that rapper was incarcerated) the show went on. T.I., Diddy, Beyoncé, Usher, Ja Rule, Snoop, and other all-stars made sure the Big Homie was good. Church!

You hear these phrases all the time: "Mind over matter." "You can do anything that you put your mind to." "Mind control." No matter what brought us to what is probably the darkest period in our lives, when we reenter society our success or failure hinges on how well we have conditioned our minds. Did we develop plans, study a vocation, battle our demons, work on skills, read, and do other things conducive to positive readjustment? Or did we just let the time do us?

I've grown a gray hair or two since my arrest in 2003. I've become a bit philosophical and sinfully optimistic. I'm a new man. And that's just perfect for a whole new world.

Mansfield B. Frazier

Accepting the Reality of One's Past

Compared to some others who have returned home from a period of incarceration, I have had a somewhat charmed life. I had an extended family with adequate, if not extravagant, resources they gladly made available to me. I wasn't saddled with an addiction or mental health problem. I also had what I felt was a salable skill—one that I'd learned in prison while serving time for manufacturing counterfeit credit cards—as a means to earn an honest living.

Since I'd been fortunate enough to publish a book, *From Behind the Wall*, in 1995, the same year I was released from Ashland Federal Correctional Institution, I thought that the world would be waiting for me with open arms. Needless to say, I was sadly mistaken.

In my first week home, I sent writing samples to every newspaper, magazine, and other type of publication within a fifty-mile radius of Cleveland, Ohio, where I'd been paroled to but had not resided for close to thirty years. I was saddened when I received only one response. But it turned out to be the right response, and the only one I needed.

Larry Durstin, the editor of a well-written and highly political monthly publication called *The Cleveland Tab,* was looking for a writer of color to add an additional perspective to the edgy journalism that he'd been publishing. My first assignment was a book review, which Durstin liked. Then, when a locally famous bail bondsman's overzealousness led to his arrest, Durstin had me write an article about the arcane world of bail bonding, which was very well received by the readership. Few people, I discovered, know the intricacies of that business as well as I do.

Within six months, I was an assistant editor with my own column, and my future was looking rosy. The owner of the news magazine hired a woman to investigate misconduct by an attorney in the county prosecutor's office. Because of my background in the criminal justice system, the owner asked me to assist her in her investigation.

Within a month, it was evident that the woman had an ulterior agenda; we discovered that she'd had a personal relationship with the attorney. By all appearances the attorney was guilty of everything that he'd been charged with and, perhaps, even more. During this period, the woman told people around town that she was "going to nail" the prosecutor in the case for misconduct, and that I was assisting her in doing so. Quite to the contrary, I'd written a report to the owner about my finding of no wrongdoing by the prosecutor. But the folks in the prosecutor's office were not aware of that report. One Friday evening, I was arrested at the offices of the news magazine on a ten-year-old charge that had been dead-docketed years before.

Dead-docketing a case is a method authorities sometimes use to keep the accused from returning to their jurisdictions to commit additional crimes. Prosecutors basically give the case a "dead" status; the charge remains but there is no arrest warrant and the authorities have no desire to prosecute—unless, of course, the accused is caught committing another crime in the area. In my case, the warrant was activated in Atlantic City, as a favor to the county prosecutor in Cleveland. It was their way of pushing back for my involvement in the investigation against the attorney. My past had come back to haunt me.

When I left prison, I had turned a mental corner. I had one thought firmly in my mind: No matter what, I would never again be on the wrong side of the law. Until a person turns that corner, he or she is subject to recidivating, something I'd done four times during my nearly thirty-year criminal career. There's no one-size-fits-all way to turn that mental corner, but certainly education is key. All studies show that the more education the incarcerated obtain, the less likely they are to recidivate, partly because they are more employable. I used to tell young guys that the only way prison doesn't just flat-out rob you of your years is if you use the time to educate yourself. One man's prison can be another man's university. Prison was my university.

And, of course, family support is critical, as is a group of peer mentors—people who've been incarcerated and have transformed their lives—who are available to offer assistance and guidance. I was fortunate enough to have both.

Yet, here I was, once again in custody, in spite of my promise to myself to never again break the law. The past, it seems, is never that far behind you.

During my career as a counterfeiter, I'd plied my trade in many jurisdictions throughout the United States. When I made my last plea bargain back in 1992 before beginning my last prison sentence, my lawyer had me plead to "all known and unknown" charges, as is customary. That would effectively prevent my being prosecuted again after my sentence was over. The plea, however, only covers federal charges. Any local charges have to be disposed of by filing a document known as an "interstate waiver on detainers." If a prisoner files the waiver, the jurisdiction holding the warrant has 180 days to come get the prisoner and take him back to face charges. If they fail to do so within the period prescribed by law, the warrant is quashed; it no longer exists. But some jurisdictions ignore the waiver so they can keep the case on the dead-docket.

So, while the local prosecutor knew that I would not face prison time for the old charge, he also knew that my having to answer the charge would cost me money for a lawyer and the trip back to Atlantic City. In fact, it cost the news magazine's owner in excess of $25,000 in bail money, lawyer fees, and travel. The New Jersey judge who heard the case knew that it had been brought against me for punitive reasons, and he was not amused. He gave the prosecutor a stern warning in open court not to bring such specious charges into his courtroom in the future. As he dismissed the case, the judge apologized to me for being subjected to such mistreatment at the hands of the judicial system. The year was 1997.

By 2007, I'd retired as the editor of a weekly urban newspaper and had been actively working in the field of prisoner reentry for three years. However, when I went to interview a person at the county jail for a reentry publication I was writing and editing, I was told there was a warrant for my arrest in Los Angeles and that, as a result, I could not enter the facility. The warrant was not active. I would not be placed in custody and shipped back to Los Angeles to answer the charge, which stemmed from a situation in 1985—twenty-two years earlier. But I would have to somehow dispose of this case. And you can't just mail it in. You have to appear in court.

Fortunately, I was scheduled to attend a White House Summit on Prisoner Reentry in the fall of 2007, and I made the trip to Washington a day early. I met the federal public defender based in Cleveland, who called the chief of the public defender's office in Los Angeles County and asked for help with my case. He mentioned my positive activities in the community and how I'd turned my life around. The L.A. chief in turn assigned a lawyer to my case. The lawyer had a discussion with the prosecutor. When I went to court, the judge simply dismissed the warrant. They can make it real simple when they want to.

Today, I still write and publish. I'm currently working on a textbook on prisoner reentry for a course that will be taught as a pilot at Case Western Reserve University in the fall of

2010. I also publish the *Reentry Advocate* magazine. But I'm always aware that my past could conceivably come back to haunt me—there could be other old charges lurking out there somewhere.

However, I don't live in fear or look over my shoulder. I've paid my debt to society for my past crimes. If people still have a problem with my past felonies, it's their problem to deal with, not mine. America is moving toward that day when former convicts will truly be given a second chance. We have an obligation to live our lives as if we truly deserve it.

John Ruzas

Reentry According to Bond

Once upon a time on a surprisingly warm December day, I took a bus ride. It was a long-anticipated ride that my mind had envisioned over many a lonely day and night. The fact that Christmas was fast approaching added a magical dimension to the trip, as I was treated to the many holiday home displays I hadn't seen in years. Even more magical was the comfort I felt because of the absence of shackles and handcuffs, which had hobbled me on every bus ride I had taken in the past four years and eight months. Complementing my comfort was the lovely dark-haired lass who sat across the aisle with a guitar, and a cast on her left wrist.

I had walked out of Green Haven state prison at 10:00 a.m. on December 12, 1972, and the bus would deliver me to "The Big Apple," for a much needed and long-denied bite.

Many years earlier—when Yogi Berra caught the fire hurled by Allie Reynolds and Rocky Marciano ruled the twenty-foot square—my teacher, Sister Mary Dennis, poked her index finger at my eleven-year-old chest and warned, "Master Ruzas, if you don't mend your ways, young man, someday you're going to wind up in one of our penitentiaries." In the spring of 1968, her fourteen-year-old prophecy became a fact, as I rode the bus to Sing Sing prison to begin a seven-year sentence. Years of reckless and feckless behavior, mixed as they were with sometime work in the construction industry as an apprentice carpenter, cabaret nights, alcohol use and heroin abuse, ended at age twenty-five, when my "stick-up" of a drugstore with an imitation pistol was interrupted by an off-duty detective with a real gun. Ouch! In the span of four years and eight months, I traveled the New York State Department of Correctional Services state prison circuit from Sing Sing to Clinton, Clinton to Attica, Attica to Comstock, Comstock to Green Haven, and Green Haven to the bus I now rode.

I had planned to spend this trip going over the list of priority "do's" I had compiled for my return from exile. The list contained a couple of phone numbers with messages from guys I had left behind, and a few promises I had given my handshake on as guarantee. Those pieces of advice that were given me by some old-timers that were credible enough to heed, I had tucked away in my mind file. I would try and find inexpensive frames for the four eight-by-ten silhouette glass paintings of Elvis and John Lennon given to me by a talented friend "inside." And, I had an intimate welcome-home date planned with an ex-honey I hadn't seen in five years. Unfortunately, as the saying goes, "Man plans and God laughs." The list never left my pocket. Instead, I sat there with the paintings on my lap, and enjoyed the fantasy that began to evolve from the waft of perfumed scent that tickled my libido from two feet away.

Thinking myself a "proper stranger" and intent upon rectifying my stranger status, I began to contemplate a successful opener, one that I hoped wouldn't devastate my sixty-eight-dollar bankroll. I considered and then dismissed the fact that I hadn't intimately or even socially interacted with a woman, young or old, in almost half a decade. Then I told myself that this was just a fantasy that would probably go nowhere, and I already had a date with Liz when the sun went down. But as the bus rolled on, I was struck by my inability to open a conversation with the dark-haired lovely to my left. I realized that it wasn't inability but reluctance that held me back.

In the past, I had never felt uncomfortable "breaking the ice" with the opposite gender, and my popularity had been early established when in the fourth grade I was the only boy invited to Diane D.'s birthday party. Could Hugh Hefner make such a claim? With the thought of fun and games fading fast, I remembered what some author had written regarding baseball and sex: "Every home run is preceded by a 'pitch.' " Still I was reluctant to make one.

After some distance-shortening minutes, marked by the awkward tongue-tied pressure I was feeling, I was forced to admit what to me was not an easy truth: My tongue was tied by fear. Fear from different angles was upon me, and it brought its cousin, insecurity, to help hold me down. Fear that the past would mar the present and hijack the future. Fear that my "Big Apple" bite might contain a white powder worm. Fear of getting off the bus in the "Land of Temptation," and returning to the same lifestyle that put me on this bus. Fear that she could smell my fear, my convict fear. Free? I'm not free. I've got a parole officer, a stranger, who's going to pull my strings, tell me where to work, who to talk to, when to come home. Who am I kidding, sitting here slickly wrapped with sixty-eight dollars in my pocket? Get real. I don't even know if I want a babe or a bag, and I really can't afford either one.

As I continued to come to grips with my reality crises, I realized that in all the time I had spent as a ward of the New York State Department of Corrections, I had never been prepared for release. Lost in that and other thoughts, I was pleasantly interrupted by a voice. "Excuse me. Did you paint those?"

"Ahh, no, no," I replied. " A friend made them for me."

"Are they all of John Lennon?" she asked.

"No. I've got two of John and two of the King."

"The King? Do you mean Elvis?"

And poof! My fear had disappeared.

I didn't ask what caused her to take the initiative, and she didn't offer. She asked if I would place her guitar in the overhead rack, and I quickly complied. After doing so, I showed her the Elvis silhouette, and she admitted to having a crush on "The King" in her teen years. She then offered, "My name is Gerry."

"Is that short for Geronimo?" I quipped.

She shook her head with a smile and said, "Geraldine. And you are?"

In my best British upper-crust imitation, I deadpanned, "Bond ... James Bond." She had a cute laugh. We talked all the way to the Port Authority Bus Terminal.

Gerry had been skiing over the weekend in Vermont and had broken her wrist. She lived in Manhattan with her boyfriend, Billy, an out-of-work ironworker. Billy was meeting her at the terminal. I liked the fact that she signaled her personal relationship right from the jump, not only because it was an immediate pressure release for me; it revealed an honesty that caused me to react in kind. The opportunity came when she asked if I skied. I told her I was better at ski jumping than downhill skiing.

When she appeared confused, I explained. "In Clinton state prison we built a ski-jump in the yard each winter. I just got out of prison this morning."

Her big brown eyes registered surprise, but no alarm. She asked how long I was away and followed that with a host of questions that for the most part were the stereotypical queries of the uninformed. But I discovered that her mind was as sharp as her face was lovely. Our banter covered a variety of subjects—music, employment (she was a dental nurse), politics and protest, movie trivia and, of course, Attica.

The 1971 Attica insurrection was still fresh in many minds. The unrest "inside the walls" was a microcosm of what was taking place in cities, suburbs, and campuses across the nation. The causes were many, as were the protests by Americans of different hue, age, and circumstance. Hippies touting free love, pot, and flower power were in protest against conventionality and the status quo's hypocrisy; Blacks had won passage of the Civil Rights Act, but four years later were protesting its slow imposition, Martin Luther King's assassination, and other grievances; college students and supporters, the Weather Underground, et al., protested the Vietnam War, and rioted at the Democratic Convention, and civil/uniformed authority was under siege.

New York's prison populations were not inoculated against the spread of protest, and they had a more immediate issue and reason to protest. Whether in disagreement or frustration with the national protest mode, or just indoctrinated in the belief that they were above the law, the prison guards—especially in Attica—were engaging in serious "beat ups" with apparent immunity. There was no means of redress, and a lethal hatred, both of which fueled the death and devastation that erupted at Attica in September 1971. Thankfully, I had been transferred from Attica to Comstock that June, but long before then I had concluded that prison was a place to get in shape, meet bad people but read good books, live confined but not corrected. In spite of the fact that approximately seventy-five to eighty percent of the men confined in its prisons suffered some form of addiction, the Department of Corrections provided no programs to help a man understand and correct his addiction. Where it is true that in response to the "Attica Armageddon" the doors to state prisons were thrown open to addiction counselors, self-help organizations, college programs, and other services, my release in 1972 meant that I could not fully participate in or benefit from them.

Arriving at the Port Authority in mid-afternoon, I saw a young guy follow the bus into the terminal. "There's Billy," I told her. She looked and waved back and forth at the window. "How did you know that's Billy?" she questioned. Again, I deadpanned, "Bond … James Bond."

When we left the bus, she introduced me to Billy, who shook my hand with the firm grip of an ironworker. He invited me for a beer and sandwich. I declined, saying that I had another appointment, to which Gerry offered a slight nod. Billy then invited me to his sister's birthday party, to take place in a Hell's Kitchen gin mill on Saturday night. I thanked him for the invite, but told him that if I didn't show up, Gerry would explain why. As we shook hands goodbye, I gave him a gift of Elvis, and wished them a Merry Christmas. Gerry thanked me with a hug, and added, "Merry Christmas to you, too, Bond, and good luck." Billy hefted both her bag and guitar, and they headed toward Ninth Avenue for their beer and sandwich.

I watched them go and thought how good they appeared for each other. Then I crossed the street to keep my appointment.

It was immediate. I no sooner walked into the building that housed the parole office, when I met Papo G, a handball-playing Latino I knew from Clinton. He had been home for two months and was already plying the profession that got him three years upstate. I would find that out and more when I had a cup of coffee with him twenty minutes later. That was my first bad decision, which would eventually be followed by many more.

I had been instructed to report to the parole office on Fortieth Street when I got off the bus. When I knocked on the door, it was answered by a little fire-breathing dragon that blew me right out of the satisfying reentry I had enjoyed. I don't remember his name, but I do remember wanting to jump across the desk and make a speed-bag out of his head. From the moment I gave him my name and release papers, his voice and demeanor caused my brain to slide downhill, for which I was totally unprepared.

During his "Captain Bligh" tirade, he announced that since I was returning to Corona, Queens, to reside at my parents' home, I would be reporting to the parole office in Kew Gardens, in another part of the borough. My parole officer's name was Nathan Grant, and I was to report to him at 3:00 p.m. the following day. I was glad that I would not be seeing "Captain Bligh" again.

I came out of the building and heard Papo G shout, "Yo! Jackie!" We went for another cup of coffee. But first, I called home to tell Mom that I had arrived okay and that I'd be home later that night. The sound of her voice and the happiness in it helped me to forget "Captain Bligh's" bullshit. It also saved me a trip down to Liz's crib. Mom said Liz had called to say she couldn't keep our appointment, but that she'd call and explain. I told Mom that in that case I'd be home soon for some Irish stew. She said okay and added that my father would be home. I hung up knowing that she had just prepared me for an "up or down" reception from my father.

Mom was my heart and best friend from my earliest memory. She was a typical Irish mother when it came to her only son. She loved me and was always there for me. She also enabled me beyond my maturation years. Were she alive today, she would endorse that claim.

My father had a real rough childhood, and he rarely expressed outward signs of love toward me, my older sister, or even Mom. The truth is that I grew up exposed to more conflict than harmony between my parents, and I always took my mother's side. But my father had been a hard worker and good provider for our family all his life. However, he never understood my reckless criminal or addictive behavior. He didn't want any part of it, or me. It was understood between us that he would not condone that lifestyle under his roof, and I always respected that because I didn't condone it either.

While Papo G and I "kicked a Willie-Bobo" about days in the joint, I was uneasy about what I felt was coming: "You wanna get high?" It dawned on me as soon as I saw that he had waited for me outside of the parole office. He was "hustling highs" from guys who were getting off the bus from prison with money in their pockets. The fact that he was living on Forty-Sixth Street and Tenth Avenue just made the hustle a good stretch of the legs from his crib. Sure enough, the offer came before I emptied my cup. I told him, "No, thanks." We finished our coffee, then he went his way and I went mine.

On the train ride home I reflected on the strange normalcy of the day. The strangeness came from living a five-year daily dependence on the state, only to be awakened this morning and shown the door. The normalcy derived from everything that took place thereafter, save for the fleeting bout of fear and paranoia I experienced on the bus. Thankfully, I had a home to go to with food in the fridge and aspirin in the medicine chest should I need one. But what about the guys who don't? What about the clean "Hopper" (heroin addict) who has nothing, no support, no money except the forty state dollars, and spends his bus ride hoping to meet a Papo G so he can get "dirty" again. That's normal to him. In the "Land of Temptation," the system provided a building where a little Captain Bligh might cause a parolee to go sniff a bag, just to feel better after meeting him, but it provided no sanctuary to help a clean addict to understand his disease and stay clean. Neither were any coping skills taught the pre-parolee that would help him deal responsibly with problems upon returning to society. I thanked Gerry and Billy for their part in my reentry, and I continued home for Mom's Irish stew.

The next day I kept my appointment with Nathan Grant, who turned out to be a decent man who happened to be a parole officer. He levied some tight restrictions on me that actually helped me walk the straight and narrow. The following Wednesday night, I attended a union meeting and Christmas party at Carpenter Local #298, where I paid the quarterly dues and was given a work permit to use until I received my union book and membership card. After a wonderful Christmas and New Year, I secured a job at a mall under construction in Queens and held it until the mall's rough construction was complete.

All in all, you could say that my reentry was a success—that is, until twenty-two months later, when I took a most tragic backslide.

On October 24, 1974, most of the newspapers in New York carried the story of a shooting on the thruway that resulted in a state trooper's death. The story contained the claim that the death penalty was in play, and most papers showed a photo of the perpetrator. Although I didn't attend the birthday party that Billy invited me to, nor did I ever see him or Gerry again, I've got a strong feeling that Gerry read the *Daily News* or *New York Post* on that lovely autumn day and loudly exclaimed, "Oh My God! Billy! It's Bond … James Bond!"

Shaun A. Bowen

Prison Came with Me

In October 2007, I went for my initial parole board interview. After serving fifteen consecutive years on a sentence of fifteen years to life for a second-degree murder conviction, I was finally going to have my first chance at freedom. I couldn't believe those years had expired and I had survived to see that day arrive.

I was nervous as I sat in the lobby rehearsing my prepared speech, and waiting for my name to be called. When my turn came, I walked in and the interview began. Sitting there, sweating from nerves, my fine-tuned speech refused to exit my brain or mouth. Instead, I answered their questions from my heart. When the interview ended, I thanked the commissioners and left.

Three days later I received the blue envelope. My first thoughts were, "Go ahead, throw it away. After all, you have a violent crime; murder, at that. No one makes their first board with a violent crime." But with shaking hands, I tore open the envelope. After looking through the Notice of Decision a couple of times, I found it: Release Date (Open): January 3, 2008.

I couldn't believe what I was reading. And then, something else hit me—what had I truly done to prepare myself? I hadn't done any networking or other preparations for my release because I never expected to go home on my first board appearance. I was expecting to serve at least twenty-five years. So, I mean, why bother, right?

I had a girl, but during the course of my incarceration she had become involved in the lifestyle I left all those years ago. Consequently, our son was taken from her and placed in foster care. When the board learned of this, I was told that I could not live with her. So I was placed in a shelter.

When my release date came, I was scared, nervous, and happy all at the same time. My stomach was in knots as I walked across the compound to draft processing with my belongings. I said goodbye, with some sadness, to those I knew. Those relationships we build in prison we are going to have to break one day. The problem is that some of us cannot break those connections.

I never knew that I personified prison until I had returned to society. I mean, for fifteen years of my life I called prison my home. It was my house and I lived there. Now, I was on my way out of my home. Little did I know that prison and all those years of jailhouse resentments were coming with me. Although I was about to traverse the streets of Syracuse, New York, as a free man, I was mentally still in prison.

I was sitting in the Utica bus station with real money in my pocket, and no correction officers or inmates. I was hungry and looked at the clock—11:00 a.m. I would be in the prison mess hall right now, I thought. Eventually, the Greyhound for Syracuse pulled up. I put my stuff in the baggage compartment and hopped on. I was so used to being told where to sit on a bus that I had to force myself to sit where I wanted. I was a stranger on this bus and felt that everyone knew I was just getting out of prison. As I looked around, though, no one was paying me any attention. As I looked at my hands, all I could think of were those waist chains, handcuffs, and that black box that goes on the cuffs. I shuffled my feet—no shackles. I wonder if I'll see a state bus, I thought to myself.

We pulled into Syracuse, and I got off the bus. Wow, civilization at last! I walked into the station and was blown away by what I saw—people, restaurants, a game room, and phones. The first thing I attempted to do was call my parole officer and let him know I had arrived at the station. I dropped a quarter in the phone, but it wouldn't connect; I later learned that I needed fifty cents, but I was too proud to ask why the phone wasn't connecting. I caught a city bus that took me downtown, and from there I went to see my P.O. for the initial interview. After that, I went to the shelter.

I figured that since I was on parole, the shelter administrators would be expecting me and I would be able to get a bed. I mean, if I was being paroled there, at least they would already have all the necessary paperwork set up, right? Boy, was I wrong. They were not expecting me; they never knew I was coming. And since it was winter, the shelter was filled to capacity. So, for about five days I had to sleep wherever I was allowed until a bed opened because someone else had not shown up. This was just like being in booking.

The shelter had four buildings—one for sleeping, another for hanging out, a mess hall, and a gym. It reminded me of prison. The lights were turned on at 6:00 a.m., and we were kicked out of the sleeping quarters at 7:00 a.m. every day, whether we were working or not. We could not return until 5:00 p.m. We would grab a meal ticket and head over to the mess hall to wait in line for breakfast.

We had to put any personal items we needed in either a duffel bag or backpack and walk around with them all day. So, I stuffed a clean shirt, towel, soap, deodorant, toothpaste, toothbrush, and Listerine strips in my backpack. There I was on the street in winter with my net bag—I mean backpack—and walking around with the little money I had saved, wondering what to do. I had gone from not having any responsibilities to being thrust out on my own—and without the luxury of three hots and a cot.

I went to public assistance and applied for welfare. I thought I would receive some type of emergency funds. Instead I was given an application, a job hunting list to fill out, and told to come back in a week with both filled out. I told them I had just come home, but their attitude was like, "So what; you're not receiving any special treatment."

So, I walked around in the winter with my backpack, filling out ten different job applications. After a week, I returned to public assistance and received a month's worth of food stamps ($147) and another form—this time with twenty different job fill-ins and a job coach interview date.

My first week felt like hell; I had blisters on both heels from walking, and I was quickly going through money. I never thought about how much more expensive it was out in society. I never had to worry about a job in prison, and the commissary was way cheaper. I had a bed to sleep in, a locker full of food, and not a care in the world. I was having a hard time adjusting.

One night I went to a small park. It was closed because of winter, but I found a bench, brushed off the snow, and cried. I couldn't hold back my frustrations and loneliness any longer. I told myself that it had to get better.

I was ready to go back to prison, to go back to being secure.

Eventually, I was hired to work nights at a Wendy's and then at an industrial laundry. Working both jobs was a bit too much so I quit Wendy's and continued working at the laundry. This job was union, and I was on a ninety-day probation before I could be unionized. Most of the employees there were foreigners, and I was ashamed of living in a shelter and having been in prison. So whenever anyone asked me about my life or where I lived, I lied.

Before I could complete the ninety-day probation period at work, I violated parole. I came oh so close to a major accomplishment, but I made a bad decision. I reconnected with my son's mother.

I didn't really know how badly she was doing. The only contact I had with her in prison was on visits or the phone, so my perception was that she was only struggling. Once I realized how bad off she was, I felt her situation was my fault. After all, I left her out there all those years to fend for herself with the kids; even though I only had one child by her, I still considered and treated the other kids as my own. So, I owed her, and I was going to fix her problem, my son's problem and mine. But my problems only became worse because I was trying to play superhero and take care of everyone but me. It was two months before I shopped for my own clothes or treated myself to a movie or dinner. And by the time I started taking care of myself, I had already built up resentments.

———⋙⋄⋘———

I had a hard time adjusting to being back in society. In order to navigate, I used the set of codes, rules, and respect I had learned in prison. For example, if I was walking into a store or restaurant and the person in front of me did not hold the door open for me, I felt offended. I would not allow myself to get caught in crowds when a bus pulled up and everyone rushed for the door. If I used a bathroom in a mall, library, or other public place and found it filthy, I became upset.

One night I took my girl to the movies and then to a Burger King for a snack. I was holding her phone while she went to the restroom. A text message of a sexual nature appeared on her phone. When I asked her what was going on, she played the dummy role. This only enraged me more. I felt violated and like I'd been played like a puppet. So, the next day I vented all my frustrations out to her and to the person who had texted her. I was going to have the last word. I mean, after all I did for her, I was not going to be played like this. I was going to fix this, and that was final!

Yeah, right! I was given thirty-six months for my threats. I am due to be released in eighteen months, but this time it's going to be a lot different. This time I will take care of me first, find some type of support, and not play the superhero.

This time I need to be a superhero to myself and, instead of trying to fix everyone else, fix myself. Also, when I return back to the land of the living, I will leave jail where jail belongs—in jail. It won't be coming home with me!

Mattie Evans Belle

This is It

This was it! I was not being released to my father, my sister, or my aunt. There was no bail—well, not one that we could afford to pay. When I say we, I mean the clean-up crew—one of them was always rescuing me from the consequences of my dysfunctional relationship with heroin. The drug either numbed me to all feelings, or familiar chills, aches, pains, and nausea accompanied me in its absence. That was my life in 1985. I was twenty-four years old and, among other things, strung out on drugs. My seven-year-old son was being raised by my mother, my aunt, my father, and my siblings.

The judge yelled, "Remand." The bailiff escorted me out of the courtroom. I turned around to look for a familiar face, and I realized there was none. I was sentenced to one year for grand larceny and a string of 155.25s—petty larcenies. I became quite familiar with the courtroom lingo and, besides, 155.25 somehow sounded better than "defendant convicted of petty larceny." It's funny when I think about it. I did not want to be known or associated with the word "petty," when in fact that is exactly what I was.

There I sat, quite comfortably I might add, in Nassau County Correctional Facility. I often wonder why these places are called correctional facilities. A more appropriate term might be "rest stop." In fact, it was there that I polished up my boosting skills. You see, the thing about jail and similar institutions is that nothing of significance is asked of you. You have to conform to the rules and regulations; however, for the most part you can continue to live out your fantasy. I am sure that there are people—in fact, I know a few of them—who, after one stint of incarceration, never return. Then, there are others like me who find a sense of comfort in those particular settings, where nothing is asked of you and, for the most part, nothing is expected. I came to rely on that and, with the exception of a spontaneous moment of clarity, I was more than comfortable; it was the rest of the world that was distorted. This type of thinking became typical, and my actions predictable. No one could trust me; moreover, I couldn't trust me.

———⟫◇⟪———

The year was 1995; my father was terminally ill and there was nothing I could do about it. By this time, I had been arrested and incarcerated several times. I had gotten married—what a tragedy that turned out to be. The week before my father died, my husband was arrested, and that was the last time I laid eyes on him. A very short time later, I, too, was arrested again. If memory serves me correctly, I was arrested on a Thursday, bailed out on a Saturday, and my dad died that following Monday afternoon while I lay drug-sick in my bed.

The guilt of not being there for my father in his last days held me hostage for many years. I remember feeling totally alone for the first time in my life. My father was the one person I could always count on and, believe me, I manipulated that fact almost up until the day he died. The thing you have to understand about an addict is that we are always the victim; it's always "woe is me." Our whole outlook on life is distorted. I sank deeper into my addiction, and in 1996 I was in a near-fatal car accident. I was totally at fault, though at the time I did not see it that way. I was not entitled to any retribution except no-fault medical insurance and, of course, I could not see the fairness of that. My only concern was who could I sue, and for how much. Never mind that I had come close to killing people, along with myself. According to witnesses and the accident report, I drove onto the exit ramp of the parkway instead of the entrance ramp while returning from one of my Long Island escapades. I woke up in Stony Brook Medical Center eleven days later, having undergone facial reconstructive surgery. I had broken nearly every bone in the left side of my face, left foot and left hip. I had also fractured my pelvis. I was informed that I was kept alive by machines for thirty-six hours. Only the grace of God had saved my life, and still I had no gratitude.

Although my primary concern was the possibility of a lawsuit, my other two concerns were whether the stolen merchandise had been recovered from the car, and whether the medical team had been informed that I was a heroin addict and would obviously need to be medicated. The emergency room team at the hospital to which I was flown by helicopter was indeed informed. Of course, when my blood work came back, there was no doubt about it. Needless to say, the accident did not bring a halt to my shenanigans.

I am not sure where the years went. I am sure, however, that for the most part, I was a no-show. It was 1997, and my son had just been arrested for assault with a deadly weapon, a fight that had gotten way out of hand. Until that moment, my attitude about everything had been take it or leave it. I was accustomed to failure, bad news, and disappointment; this, however, was entirely different. My son was my promise of all good things.

As I sat across from him in the visiting room, the fear that I saw in my son's eyes chilled me to the bone. He was scared, and I was scared for him. For the first time in I don't know how long, I wanted to put him first; he deserved to be put first. He was allowed three visits a week; one was reserved for me, one for my aunt who had become his legal guardian and who was also the only mother figure he had known, and one for his girlfriend. I made regular visits until eventually I, too, was once again incarcerated. This time I was facing another state sentence for grand larceny. I say another because in 1989, while visiting my brother in Chicago, I found myself in Dwight Correctional Facility for grand larceny. I served eighteen months.

I was sentenced to six months to three years on April 9, 1998. Coincidentally, my son received the same sentence. My sister died two weeks later and, because of a technicality, I was unable to attend the viewing or the funeral. I am not exactly sure if it was not being able to say goodbye to my sister, or my son being incarcerated in a state penitentiary, but I had a spiritual awakening. What had happened to my life? How had it all gone so terribly wrong? For the first time in I don't know how long, I was actually giving some thought to my life.

The first few months of that stretch were really tough. My brother and my son were in state facilities. In order for us to communicate by way of the postmaster, we each had to obtain permission from the state via our counselors. By May I received my first letter from my brother; June and July passed by without any word from my son. I knew from the home front that he was doing okay and making the best of things; however, there was nothing from him. I spoke with my counselor and she assured me that permission was granted. I finally heard from my son in October.

The letter, the words, were a long time coming. They contained all the emotions that he could not articulate at the tender ages of four, five, seven, and eight, his adolescence and formative years, because I was off doing me, and he was there trying to make sense of it all. I had always prided myself in showing up, with outfits for him to boot; I had always been able to fall back on the fact that I showed up—if I wasn't incarcerated—for all family functions.

In his letter, he let me know how very disappointed he was in me. He was tired of protecting my feelings. He did not want a mother who showed up on occasion with a bag full of clothes and a couple of dollars; he wanted his mother to be the woman he believed I could be. He said that he believed his words would reach me because they came straight from his heart. In fact, he said simply that if his sentiments did not move me to change, then he would change his feelings toward me. Actually, what he said was that he would move on with his life minus me.

Well, I am not sure what happened, and why it had not happened nineteen years earlier, but what my son thought of me now meant something. It meant enough for me to consider doing something different, for the first time.

Then, a couple of months later, I heard from a girlfriend of mine with whom I had done the better part of my bid. When she was paroled in August 1998, she had promised to send a package with some delicious goodies. This is what usually happens when someone that you have forged an alliance with goes home before you do. It's street ethics. I was in solitary confinement Christmas Eve, and I received a letter from her with a fifty-dollar money order, and talk of a new way of life. She had cleaned up her act and wanted me to know that the only reason that I had not heard from her with the promised goodies was because she no longer engaged in such things. While we had talked about that particular bid being hard, we had never really resigned to do anything else. She sent regards from friends whom I had not heard from in years; she had run into them at the self-help meetings she had begun making. Some of these people were like me, heavily vested in the life of crime and all that it entails.

I remember one night shortly after that; I was lying on my bunk thinking to myself that maybe I, too, could find a new way of life. The truth is, I cannot recall if that was the thought or if it was more like, "This whole show is becoming a drag." Whatever it was, it was one more thing that made me think about doing things a different way.

Initially, I was not certain what that "different" would be. However, I figured that for starters I would go straight home upon my release instead of seeing what was going on in the streets.

On April 29, 1999, I was paroled to my mother's house, under protestation from my siblings and some might say against her better judgment. My mother did what most mothers do; she opened up her heart and home without reservation. Well, let's be realistic—there was probably some reservation. Nonetheless, I was home. I was committed to doing things differently. I went from point A to point B with no detours; I was learning to survive my feelings of anxiety and fear. My mother was visibly happy to see me; I shared a drink or two with her and the streets weren't calling me.

I was home and had to adhere to a few parole stipulations if I wanted to stay in the free world. For starters, I was to enroll in an outpatient program where I was expected to show up without fail, five days a week; in addition, I was to attend twelve-step meetings regularly. The parole board explained that I was one year shy of being deemed a career criminal, and while my arrest record was lengthy, it was clear to them that my problems were really rooted in drugs and/or alcohol. Needless to say, I took offense at their findings because, up until then, it had always been the town, the county, and the people I was hustling with that were the problems. To even consider that it may be the drugs seemed far-fetched.

But I knew that some things were going to have to change if I was going to honor my son's feelings. I just did not know what that something would be. There had been countless detoxification episodes, and one feeble attempt at a rehabilitation center that was similar to a resort—my stay there was all of forty-eight hours. I had even attended a meeting way back when, but those folks were squares who had lost the ability to keep up their hustle—unlike me who could always be counted on to get the party started. I had no concept of the recovery process or how staying sober would impact my life. I did know, though, that my life had become completely unmanageable, and that I hadn't the faintest idea of how to get it all together. Then again, that is not entirely accurate. I knew that there was one who could help when no one else could, and that one was God.

I came from a family that believed in the power of prayer, and I, too, had a personal relationship with God. I knew that he was the Alpha and Omega. The prayer I prayed was no parting-of-the-Red Sea kind of prayer; in fact, I cannot recall exactly what I prayed. I just knew that I had to give this new way of living a shot and, if I was going to stand a chance, I had to actively participate.

The transition did not happen overnight. But I began to see evidence of a new way of life in what the people at the meetings were sharing. And I felt comfortable with my outpatient counselor right from the start. I felt compelled to be honest with this woman, who reminded me of the sitcom star Donna Reed. My relationship with my parole officer was open and honest, too. When I was paroled in April 1999, I did not immediately stop using; I had no idea how to do that. I needed to be taught. The people in the meetings would say, "Don't use; make a meeting and talk about how you feel."

I bought into the concept wholeheartedly and began doing just that. I made those meetings faithfully. I went from being a habitual criminal and a high school dropout to a tax-paying citizen and a college graduate. I remember when I first went back to school, I felt so inadequate; I took the entrance exam three times before passing it.

I knew that human service was my true vocation; however, what I did not know was that I would be rendering services to people much like myself who had given up on the possibility of happiness and contentment. I went from being a state inmate to a state employee, as a substance abuse counselor. I have been blessed with an occupation that allows me, on a daily basis, to give back what was so freely given to me—an opportunity to grow to my full potential.

I can clearly recall the days when my claim to fame was notoriety in the world of low-level crime; now I live to survive my feelings day to day. My son, who gave me an ultimatum, has also given me three beautiful grandchildren (the oldest reports that I make the best waffles in the world). We have a relatively productive relationship; we still struggle with certain issues, or I struggle with forgiving myself for the past.

There are good and bad days. There are things about my life that I have come to terms with, and then there are things in my life that still baffle me and I find difficult to understand. I have come to terms with the fact that I may never understand. What is important is that I work on it a day at a time. I have accepted responsibility for the part I've played and the damage I have caused. There are some things that I can only make amends for by not ever doing them again, and by empowering people who struggle with some of the same issues that I had.

I have moved on. I can no longer hold myself or others hostage with guilt and shame, regrets, and confusion—and that was a process. My greatest challenge was my relationship with my family, specifically my son. Al Green's song said it best—"How Do You Mend a Broken Heart?" Contrary to popular belief, time does not always make the heart grow fonder, nor does it heal old wounds; you have got to do that yourself. I had to gain my family's trust again.

How did I accomplish that when I never learned to trust myself? Fortunately, my son made that easy. As it turned out, he really was my biggest fan. I think that the biggest hurdle I needed to get over was my own guilt. How could I forgive myself when I had held on to so many resentments? The opportunity presented itself for me to face my life, with all its flaws. I knew that this God-given moment of total forgiveness might not come again.

This moment of clarity came with a host of gifts: a renewed sense of hope and serenity. Most important, for the first time since I could remember, impending doom was not some overwhelming sidekick. In fact, I began to look forward to life, not dread the mere thought of it. The glass was actually beginning to look half full. This was a direct result of the meetings of self-help groups I had begun attending. It was there that I heard countless stories of people who had basically suffered from the same feelings of worthlessness and self-pity as I had. It was home, a safe place for the lost, now found.

It has been a little over ten years since that long-time-coming spiritual awakening. And while life still brings its highs and lows, I find it all the more worth living. I have had to face the unemployment, breakups, untimely deaths, and health issues; however, I also faced the births of my three grandchildren, reconciliations with family members, and newfound friendships. I have done all of this without the use and abuse of any illicit substances.

Today, I present myself to the world as a productive, tax-paying member of society. I do not dwell in the past. I may visit it; however, I do not romanticize it. I face it and accept my decisions. I know that all the decisions I've made have subsequently afforded me the life that I live now.

I once heard someone say that it is as if they have been blessed with two lives in one lifetime, and I totally identify.

Anything is possible. All that was lost can be found.

Jonathan M. Petty

Revolving Doors (The Story of My Life)

Some call it rehabilitation; others call it corrections. As I stood there on my release day with thirty-four dollars and eighty-three cents in my hand from the Pennsylvania Department of Corrections, I called it neither.

As the final four-inch-thick steel door that separated me from my loved ones, my future, and my destiny began to inch its way open, I looked myself over—from my brown state boots to my blue button-down shirt that was so thin it could have been made from handkerchief cloth. The shirt was too small for my 350-pound, five-foot-nine body; I couldn't even button it.

The door banged to rest, and I walked to freedom accompanied by three other men who were also being released and a correctional officer, who drove us to the nearest Greyhound station. During my three-and-one-half-year incarceration, I was called Cleve, short for Cleveland. Before I was incarcerated, I was called Big Mike. Armed with my new certificates in accounting, payroll procedures, typing, and entrepreneurship, I entered the free world as Jonathan M. Petty, a thirty-year-old African-American male.

Four hours and fifteen minutes later, I could feel the anxiety building in my body as the sky outlined the city that I loved and missed so much in the last few years—Cleveland, Ohio. This was the city that raised me because my parents wouldn't; the city that made me the man that I am, although I don't know if that's really a blessing or a curse. My mind raced as I stared out the bus window at familiar sights and streets that had allowed me to eat and make a living for myself as a young teen—until I was sentenced in 2002.

I asked myself whether I was truly done with the drug life: "If times get hard, can you really suppress the urge to pick up a gun and rob the first person you can find with a nice stash of cocaine?"

I answered, "Yes, I have what I need to get a job. Mom gave me a room in her new house, and I have my faith in God to help me with the rest. Yeah, I can do this."

The bus driver announced our arrival at the downtown Greyhound station. I grabbed my brown paper bag and walked into the terminal that I knew so well from smuggling drugs to a couple of small towns in Pennsylvania. I no longer recognized the once prostitute-infested, rundown bus station where you could easily buy the drug of your choice. It had been drastically remodeled and cleaned up. Armed security guards walked the grounds and glanced at the Browns game on the newly installed televisions positioned above the waiting area. "Man, this place has changed!" I thought to myself. I walked over to the payphones and reached into my pocket for the one dollar and seventy-five cents I had left after buying my bus ticket. I dropped two quarters in the slot and dialed my number. After the third ring, my mom answered the line.

"Hey, Ma, I'm home! I'm at the bus station. Can you pick me up?" She told me that she was glad I was home and that she was on her way. I figured it would take her about forty-five minutes. Having been confined for more than three years, I decided to wait outside in the front and enjoy the city air.

Ten minutes later, I felt the vibrations before I heard them. A pearl white, four-door 1995 Fleetwood Cadillac, with a mint green rag top, twenty-inch rims, and a heavy beat in the trunk turned the corner and pulled up right in front of the station, shaking its glass windows. The sight of that car made me feel that I was really home and back in the thick of things.

When I got locked up, everybody was still putting hundred-spoke gold Daytons on their rides. Cats had definitely stepped up their game. Could I possibly do the same by giving the game up? That fast, I was second-guessing my plan. I hadn't thrown my plan out the window, but I now realize that that Cadillac was the trigger on the gun that could blow away my successful legal reintegration into society. I had unconsciously put my finger on the trigger.

When Mom finally pulled up, I noticed she had brought along two passengers—my niece, Erica, and her girlfriend.

Before I was locked up, Erica had been curious about the same sex. I guess she liked it and went all out as a lesbian. Man, how things can change in a few years. I hugged Mom and Erica, and then Erica introduced me to her girl, Lady. Now, Lady wasn't Halle Berry, but she was the prettiest, thickest woman I had seen in three-and-a-half years. The sight of her double-D cleavage gave me an instant erection. But Lady was my niece's girl, so I didn't even think about flirting with her.

When we pulled off the freeway and into a neighborhood I knew all too well, I wondered again if I could resist the temptations of living in the middle of my 'hood, my stomping grounds—130th and Bellaire, a small place on this earth that I swore I would always be loyal to and represent until my death. I couldn't wait to get out and see my homies and the females—the same people I had told myself during my incarceration I wasn't even going to speak to because they didn't show the support I wanted when I needed it.

We pulled into the driveway of a two-story red brick abode with a nice front lawn and a small front porch. Mom said, "This is it; you like it?" I told her it was very nice and that I was glad she finally had a house to call her own. All three women ushered me inside and gave me a tour of the two-bathroom, two-bedroom home with an attic that doubled as my mom's bedroom, and a basement that was set up as an extra family room. The last stop on the tour was my bedroom. Erica walked over to the closet and opened it so I could see the space packed with new clothes hanging up and boxes of new sneakers on the floor.

"Surprise!" Mom said. "We went shopping for you." She then opened the dresser drawers and showed me all the boxer shorts, color t-shirts, socks, doo-rags of all colors, and the jail mail I had sent home from prison. I was speechless. I was so used to doing everything for myself that I didn't expect to get anything from anybody. The look on my face must have told them how I felt. My mother hugged me and welcomed me home. She and Erica had thought this would help me.

"'Thank y'all so much," I said. "This has surprised the hell out of me." We all started laughing. Mom told me to take a shower and put on some real clothes so we could go to a buffet she liked and get some food.

I went to the bathroom and gave my facial hair a touch-up with the clippers and took a shower. I put on a Polo t-shirt, Polo jean shorts, and the Polo tennis shoes that matched the outfit. I broke open a black doo-rag and put it on because my braids were old.

At the restaurant, Mom, Erica, Lady, and I ate, talked, and joked about my jail stories and the things that happened in the streets while I was gone. The place had a small bar, so Erica, Lady, and I had a drink after we ate. It was Erica's treat. She ordered three shots of Grey Goose and three Heinekens. Erica pulled out about a thousand dollars to pay for the drinks. I was shocked.

I took a sip of my beer, and with a smirk on my face I asked, "What you been doing, niece?"

"Trying to get at a dollar—the same thang you about to be doing, unc," she said.

"Naw, I gotta get a job this time so the parole people won't be trippin'," I responded.

"That's good and all; wish you luck finding one," she said, raising her Grey Goose and toasting me. "To unc. I'm glad you home!"

We drank and talked and then Erica pulled out a small glass jar with a big pretty bud in it, looked at me and said, "You smokin'?" Now, anybody who knew me before the last three-and-a-half years knew I didn't give a damn about probation or parole when it came to smoking weed. I was gonna smoke and try to beat the urine test, or I just wouldn't go see my parole officer if I knew I was gonna test positive for marijuana. But, I told myself, "No weed this time around. I'm staying focused and sticking to my plan." I just told Erica, "I can't smoke, niece. I gotta see my P.O. tomorrow."

Later that evening, my cousin Deon came by the house to pick me up. Erica had given me $200 pocket money and a bottle of Grey Goose she had stashed at my mom's house. I wasn't surprised to see that Deon was doing his thang, too. He pulled up in a 2004 cherry red Monte Carlo with heavy beat in the trunk. He jumped out, left the music blasting and said, "What up, Boss?" He hugged me and dapped me up. The reason Deon called me Boss is because I'm an aspiring rap artist along with his older brother, Black Boob. Black Boob got sent to prison a year before I got out and had another six months to go, so the rap game was on hold.

Deon said, "Let's roll," and we got into the car. Before we pulled out of the driveway, he changed the CD and said, "This is some stuff Boob was working on while you were gone. He wanted you, the Chronic Boss, to put some verses to the tracks."

I told him, "Let it bang." He turned the volume way up and we pulled off.

We drank a little as we rode through the neighborhood and listened to Black Boob's CD. After a while, we pulled into Emery Park and, as usual, the place was packed with cats from my block. Everybody was drinking and smoking weed, shooting dice and making the same transactions that got me locked up in the first place.

The first test I knew I had to face was seeing if the lifestyle was truly out of my system. I had to know if I was "rehabilitated," if my mind had been "corrected," as they say. When we got out of the car, there was nothing but love and genuine happiness that I was home. People I had done a lot of dirt with and close friends were all there. There were so many daps and hugs, I wanted to say, "Where were y'all for the past three-and-a-half years?" But the thoughts vocalized into something different: "Y'all know I just got out today and my pockets is hurting; what you got for me?"

After making rounds around the Westside, stopping at friends' and family's houses, bars, and the hotel Deon had lined up with a couple of chicks, we pulled into my mother's driveway at about 4:00 in the morning. I was drunk but I hadn't hit one blunt or done anything I considered illegal. I had a key, so I let myself in as quietly as possible.

I went to my room and closed the door. I emptied all of my pockets on the bed, took a step back, and looked at the blocks of crack and the bills of money I now had in my possession—welcome home gifts from friends and family. I still felt no pressure to sell dope again so I told myself I'd give it to Erica and Deon. All the blocks equaled about two ounces of crack. I stuffed it into a pair of socks and put it in the drawer. The money looked like more than it was—$375— and my niece had given me $200 of that. It's a trip in the 'hood how friends and family can't afford to give you money in a time of need but can give you $2,000 worth of drugs. I put the money on the dresser, turned the radio on low, and laid back and went to sleep.

I woke up the next morning around 10:30 a.m. I took a shower and got dressed. Mom had already left for work so I fried a couple of eggs and some bacon, ate breakfast, then left to catch the bus downtown to see my parole officer.

I sat in the waiting area for about an hour and a half for my P.O. to come back from lunch. She gave me the usual rundown—stay out of trouble, get a job, and don't change my address without notifying her first. I had to pay a twenty-five-dollar supervision fee, and I put twenty-five dollars on my fines and court cost. I took a urine test and was given an appointment card for thirty days later. I left the parole office in search of a job. I bought a local newspaper and went straight to the classifieds.

By the end of the business day, I had ridden ten buses to fill out five job applications. The next three weeks went by in a blur of job applications, buses, follow-up phone calls to jobs that never got back to me, and late nights kicking it with my cousins Deon and Dre.

I could tell that my mother was regretting her decision to let me stay with her because she was really pressing my job situation, to the point it was hurting more than it was helping. On top of that, she tried to give me a 7:00 p.m. curfew. Things really changed for the worse when my mother decided to let my sister Angie come stay with us. Angie had a bad crack habit, but she convinced my mom that she had stopped and wanted to get back on her feet.

Things went smoothly for a couple of days. I even went to one of those temporary job agencies that pay you the same day. My sister would go with me. We had to get up at 4:00 a.m. and walk from our house on 130th down to Ninety-Sixth Street. The buses didn't run that route so early in the morning so the walk took about an hour one way. My sister was always sent on a job because the people there knew her. When it came to me, I walked that walk for seven days and never got sent to one job.

By now, Mom was hinting that I should find somewhere else to live because she didn't have the money to support me.

It was a blessing the day I got a phone call for an interview the following day. Mom seemed genuinely happy for me.

I took my braids out and pulled my Afro into a neat ponytail. I picked out the appropriate clothing—a white buttoned shirt, black slacks, and a pair of black loafers. The interview was for a sales position in a small company. I thought that with my personality and people skills I would nail the position. I thought wrong. The interview went extremely well. At the end, I just knew the interviewer was gonna ask, "When can you start?" But, instead, I knew he was trying to let me down easy when he said they may have a position in the near future and would give me a call if they could use me. Feeling defeated, I walked out of the office.

I caught the bus and got home at around 11:00 a.m. My sister was in the shower and Mom was at work. I was about to give up my job search, but something in me said, "Don't quit." I started calling every place where I had filled out applications.

My sister interrupted me and asked if I was going to be home. I told her I was going back out and I'd be gone for a while. She asked to borrow my house key because she was going to a job interview and would be back before me. I gave it to her without a thought. She said she had to leave in twenty minutes so I should be ready to leave, too, so we could lock the house.

I changed into some comfortable clothes and grabbed some socks to put on. They were heavier than usual. Then it hit me—the two ounces of crack. I had totally forgotten it, probably because I was drunk when I stashed it in the socks. I pulled it out and stared at it. I thought to myself, I don't even have bus fare. I opened up a block, broke off two twenty-dollar chunks, and put away the rest.

Angie and I left the house and went our separate ways. By the time I had walked three blocks deeper into my neighborhood, I had sold both chunks of crack and had forty dollars in my pocket. I got change at the corner store and went to the bus stop.

That day, I filled out four more applications at restaurants, including Burger King. I called my cousin Dre from my last stop and he came and picked me up. We talked about life and thangs. Then he told me that if I was ready to get on my grind, he had a spot for me and whatever I needed. I didn't accept, but I didn't turn him down either.

When he dropped me off, it was about 9:30 p.m. Mom went crazy when I walked in the house. "Where you been, Michael? Why the hell did you leave my house unlocked like that? Give me my damn key back! From now on, if your ass ain't in here by 7:30, the doors will be locked and your ass ain't getting in. You out there running the streets and ain't thinking about no job."

I tried to explain what I'd been doing and what I'd been going through with the job search. But when I told her Angie and I had locked the house and left together, and that I had given Angie my key, she told me to take my stuff and leave because Angie must have come back and left the house unlocked when she went back out. As a matter of fact, she said we both had to go. She would deal with Angie's crack-smoking ass whenever she came back.

I was so mad I didn't even argue. I packed my stuff and called Dre to come pick me up. I told him what happened and he said he'd be there in ten minutes.

When Dre got there, I put my stuff in his car and told him to take me to the spot he had for me. He was cool with that, but he didn't have any dope then. I showed him my stash and said, "I got some already."

An hour and a half later, I sat at the kitchen table of the dope spot with a loaded .38 snub nose in my pocket and a razor blade in my hand cutting up an ounce of crack.

I had given up. I gave in to what I knew like the back of my hand. I felt natural, like a lion in the jungle. I hadn't been rehabilitated or corrected. All those programs and educational classes ended up meaning nothing when they didn't work and I was faced with adversity. My reentry into society as a law-abiding citizen had failed.

I could blame it on not having the support I needed. I could blame it on not having financial assistance from the government. I could blame it on a lot of things. The truth is I tried, but I didn't try hard enough. No amount of programming or so-called reprogramming will work if you don't truly come to terms with yourself and what you want your life to be about. From the time you're born you start to learn, and for some of us the values and way of life that we are taught over and over again don't mesh with the values and laws of society.

I was arrested one month later because I sold a twenty-dollar rock to an undercover officer. I was held for seventy-two hours and released. I was told that I may or may not be indicted because they couldn't find the marked twenty on me. I gave them a phony address and went on my way.

I got on my feet quickly. I purchased a new Audi and an apartment in suburban Berea. Six months later I got into a heated argument with my girlfriend outside our apartment. Neighbors called the police, and when they came, they ran my name. It came back with a warrant for a drug charge. That's how I learned they'd indicted me for making the sale to the undercover officer.

I was sentenced to six months of state time in Ohio. But since my parole had been transferred to Ohio from Pennsylvania, after I did my six months, I was extradited to

Pennsylvania—back to the same prison I had left. I ended up serving fourteen more months for parole violations before I was again standing in front of that four-inch-thick steel door, slowly inching its way open.

David Stephenson

A Father's Return

E ach dorm here at the prison resembles a giant warehouse that is subdivided into fifty units, or "cubes." If you were to send me a letter, you would address it to Marcy Correctional Facility, Dorm E-1, #24, as opposed to my former address of 6436 Emerald Circle. It is an area six feet by ten feet. The cubicle walls are metal and painted a light tan that contrasts minimally with the eggshell concrete walls of the edifice. The walls are only four feet high, and reach about halfway between my belly button and pecs. Privacy is one of the first casualties of prison life.

I guess you could say that I have been involuntarily downsized from a two-story house with a two-car garage on an acre lot to this small space, not quite the size of my former walk-in closet. But it's not as if I need a lot of space anymore. Before

I got sentenced, I signed over all of my property to my ex-wife, who would be going without child support during my six-year term of imprisonment. The house was repossessed, along with my twenty-nine-foot motor yacht and Z71 truck. The rest of my property was sold at an estate sale at bargain prices, I hear. I hope whoever got the hot tub will enjoy it at least half as much as I would right now.

The cube comes with a metal frame bed with a two-inch mattress, a single chair, and two lockers—one big and one small. The small locker holds my state prison uniforms, known as "state greens," socks, underwear, and a few personal items of clothing. The big locker holds my winter clothes: a green state-issued jacket, two hoodies, some thermal underwear, and sweatpants and tops. The latter is a staple of everyday wear around here, where there is no one to impress. On the left side of the locker, I have some books, legal papers, personal hygiene items, linen, and a Walkman radio. Rounding out the extent of my property are a lamp clipped to the rail at the head of my bed and a fan. The fan has seen better days. It was sent in a package from my sister when I first came "Up North" to prison. In prison parlance it is "twisted": the cover is in tatters, the clip-on device is busted, and the wiring is temperamental. But it still came in handy last July during a hot spell.

Every Monday morning, Sergeant Newman, a short, squatty figure with a shiny pate like a glow ball, comes around for inspection. There is to be nothing on top of the lockers, our beds have to be made, and our shoes placed orderly at the foot of the bed. In addition, the floors have to be swept and mopped. In all, it is about a two-minute job for such a small area. Sometimes Newman writes misbehavior reports for untidiness, and I have seen guys lose their recreation and commissary privileges for a week over the matter. The way I keep my cube is so-so: not too bad to get a ticket, but bad enough to get a verbal reprimand now and then. "You need to get your cube in compliance," he is always saying. His attitude seems to be that one should take pride in where he lives.

I spend a lot of time in my cube listening to National Public Radio through headphones, reading, and especially thinking about all the years of training and education I have thrown away. It took me decades to develop the ability to diagnose acute medical problems, fix complex wounds, and put in chest tubes. I have traded that livelihood for a prison job where I make twenty cents an hour. I clean the officers' bathroom and type the daily dorm roster.

Fortunately, the regular dorm officer likes me. He often gives me the local newspaper, a granola bar, or sometimes a taste of home-cooked food. Whenever his luck is good at the casino, he may bring a treat like donuts, a chalupa from Taco Bell, or a Whopper. In prison, major delights come in small packages. I think he likes the fact that I have a sense of humor, and that I do not get mad when he is always busting my balls. He never seems to tire of kidding me about all that I am missing out on: "Hey, Doc, did I tell you about the retro paycheck and pay raise I'm getting in October?" "The economy in decline? Yeah, right," he often brags. Or he may mention the snowmobile he just bought, or an upcoming vacation.

He has a hard time believing I was a doctor. He frequently will ask where all the money went because I never get packages or money from home. The truth is, I signed over most of my remaining property, after paying my legal bills, to the mother of my kids. When something is offered from a family member, I tell them to send money to my kids.

Prison is supposed to be punishment for those who have violated the laws; the fact is, in my case, it is not hard being humble or having a regular routine, even at menial work. But the boredom can be depressing. It was hard working twelve-hour shifts in the emergency room, where the demands can be overwhelming and the delivery of bad news constant. Hard is working yourself ragged, not getting a day off, and then having to pay too much in taxes.

I am by no means implying that I am comfortable here; I do not want to spend one second longer here than I have to. But I have noticed an irony. In prison there is very little in the way of free choice, but a lot of free time. In the real world there is much free choice, but no free time. Before, I made a good living and had all the advantages of a free society, but I never had the leisure time to immerse myself in books like *Moby Dick* and *Oliver Twist*.

If I could make just one point to Lady Justice it would be that it is often the children who suffer the most when they have an incarcerated parent. Kids should have parents around to see the important milestones in their lives. These times can never be made up. The day Daryn was to start his first day of school, I wanted to be there, but there was absolutely nothing I could do to make that happen. I was only left to imagine how brave he must have looked getting on the bus that first time. That day, I cried.

Once I am released in a few months, the kind of life I can provide for my sons may depend on whether I get my medical license back. My former attorney told me it would be possible, but I think he was just trying to get me to take the plea. I had a defense for giving prescriptions to the undercover cop without giving him a physical exam. Just because it happened over the Internet does not make it in bad faith. The Department of Health was not willing to entertain that argument, and the state was intent on making an example of the first doctor to be prosecuted for prescribing over the Internet.

It is hard to watch all those years of education and training go to waste. At forty-eight years old, I have developed no other skills. But I can learn to live with the loss of income and property. It is the shame of being marked as a criminal in the eyes of my two sons that is the worst thing. A shame made worse each of the last three Father's Days, when they came to visit and the signs of their hardship were on their faces.

No matter what happens with my career, I am grateful that I still have them to look forward to. I have been out of their lives for almost five years now. What are their interests and talents? Their mom communicates very little about them. When I am released, I will work hard to find out for myself. I have visions of using my tutoring skills, developed while I was a teacher's aide in prison, to help them with their homework. I might even get involved in the PTA, if they let ex-convicts do such things. If the boys are interested in baseball, basketball, or football, I will be there playing catch, shooting hoops, or throwing long touchdown passes. If they prefer music over sports, I will make sure they get proper instruction and practice. No matter if they score a winning goal, march in a band competition, or bake a winning cake, I will be a proud father.

Each cube has a designated area on the dividing wall where inmates are allowed to hang personal items. A lot of guys hang artwork or pictures of their families and friends. Some of the young guys hang nude photos. One inmate two cubes down from me, who goes by the nickname Y. G., is always hanging pictures of his "new girlfriends" that he has collected from *Buttman Magazine*. His initials stand for Young Gangster, stemming from a reputation on the streets as a stick-up kid. Now, at age forty-one, he has twenty years in and another ten to go before he is released. I have heard the guards tease him with the initials G. O., for game over.

I only have two pictures hanging in my cube: school photos of my two boys. Their smiles have lost some of the gleam and their hair is a tad bit long. Daryn has a closed tight-lipped smile, which I know is hiding a cavity in need of repair. Some of Dylan's blond hair is astray. Their cleaned and pressed shirts tell me that their mom is doing the best she can without the child support. These two small faces give me all the strength and determination I need to make it through this bid and to remain on the straight and narrow path from now on.

Dean A. Faiello

The Phoenix

I was nervous. A clammy sweat formed under my state-issued green shirt. Armed only with a broken piece of chalk, I walked to the blackboard at Attica's Transitional Services Center. As I began to write, groans and catcalls erupted from the guys seated in the classroom.

"Yo, Teach, it ain't that serious."

"Why do I gotta take this class?"

"What time is the go-back?"

I wrote a seemingly incongruous list of names on the blackboard—Nelson Mandela, Viktor Frankl, St. Paul, and Martin Luther King, Jr. As I wrote the last name, the din began to subside. Dr. King often had that effect. I turned to face the class.

"Each of these men has something in common with the others. Anybody know what it is?" The classroom quieted down more as the guys realized they didn't have the answer. "Each of these men has been imprisoned, and wrote about it. Not only that, but their experiences in jail, and their writings, have changed the course of world history."

My confidence returned when I spoke those words. I began my lecture about the power of prison writing.

I explained that Nelson Mandela wrote *Long Walk to Freedom*—a walk that took twenty-seven years to complete. At his inauguration as president of South Africa in 1990, his jailers, sitting in the front row, cried as they realized the magnitude of the event, and their wrongs.

After his imprisonment in a Nazi concentration camp during World War II, Viktor Frankl, an Austrian psychiatrist, wrote *Man's Search for Meaning*. At the start of the war, he was forcibly taken from his home, along with his wife and daughter, and pushed into a cattle car on a train bound for Auschwitz. When the train car doors were flung open, the Nazis herded the men to the right, and the women to the left. He never saw his family again. His book explains how he survived and what he learned from the experience. He wrote: "We give our suffering meaning by the way in which we respond to it." Pain and suffering are inevitable. But the misery they bring is optional.

Martin Luther King, Jr.'s famous essay, "Letter from a Birmingham Jail," was written in a prison cell in Alabama. He was arrested at a peaceful civil rights protest. After his jailers refused to give him pencil and paper, he started his essay with a borrowed pencil on scraps of newspaper found in his cell. Prison officials finally admitted his attorneys, who gave him pen and paper. The resulting essay stands as one of the most powerful pieces ever written on racial equality and human rights. It can be found in collections of the best essays of the twentieth century.

"If anybody wants to read 'Letter from a Birmingham Jail,' we have a copy in the Transitional Services Library," I said. One hand went up. "I'll get it for you after the class. Anybody know what a recidivist is?"

"Yeah, that's when your P.O. violates you."

"Or a new bid. A recidivist is someone who comes back to jail after being released."

Not only was St. Paul the Disciple imprisoned, I told the men, but he was also a recidivist. He didn't learn his lesson the first time. Jailed in Caesarea for his religious beliefs, he wrote four of the letters in the Bible. His letters, known as the "Captivity Epistles," have profoundly affected the lives of millions of Christians. He didn't let his unjust imprisonment affect his attitude toward life. Whether jailed or free, he showed love to his fellow man in all his actions.

Over two million Americans are incarcerated. But not one of them should be ashamed. Malcolm X said, "There is no shame in being a criminal. The shame is in staying one." Learning nothing from one's mistakes, not even trying to change, is a sad waste of a life. To those willing to learn, incarceration can be an empowering, life-altering event. Change is difficult and hard-won. It can be painful and frightening because it requires confronting the unknown. But the process can make one stronger and smarter.

I told the class the story of the Egyptian mythological bird, the Phoenix. Every five hundred years, the bird renews his quest for his true self. He knows this can be achieved only by letting go of his bad habits, tired defenses, and failed beliefs. Bravely, he builds a funeral pyre with cinnamon and myrrh. Without hesitation, he enters the flames.

From the ashes of his destruction, the Phoenix is reborn—wiser and more powerful. Each one of us can do the same if we confront our fears. We must let go of our tired thinking, and the problems it brings, and venture down a new path. From the shattered pieces of a life, we can bravely confront change. Viktor Frankl's life was shattered. Although in pain, he moved on and rebuilt his life.

⟫◆⟪

Sometimes I sit in my cell and think about what brought me here. Like the Phoenix, I'm on a quest—to deal with loss. We all experience it; it is inevitable. But the misery that loss can bring is optional. We each have the power to choose what we do with our loss and the pain it brings.

I used my pain to justify drinking and drugging. Eventually, I grew tired of self-medicating. It's temporary and fleeting. Every time I sobered up, the pain was still there, only deeper and more devastating. It took me many years, with much loss and suffering for my family, before I reached bottom.

When I got locked up, I started my recovery. I intend for it to sustain me long after reentering society. Part of my rehabilitation is writing. Through my writing, I look at my pain. Closely. At times with a microscope. It is a slow, laborious process, as any microscope-gazing researcher will tell you. But the underlying structure that supports the pain is slowly coming into focus. At times it's frightening and ugly, but it gives me the strength to face the darkest days.

Many times I thought being locked up was a waste—pointless, futile, and senseless. But I learned that incarceration can be a strength, an advantage, if you confront it head-on. For example, during a job interview, address the issue honestly. Explain what happened. Not excuses, simply the events, the mistakes you made, and what you learned from those mistakes. Talk about what you discovered about yourself, about how to deal with stress, and how to resolve problems, not ignore them. If you can survive and grow in prison, you can thrive anywhere. Explain to a potential employer how you have turned adversity into a blessing.

Let go of the shame. If you talk openly about a secret, you take away its power. It's out in the open where you can deal with it. Go to support groups and talk about your experience. Open up at twelve-step meetings. Talk with young people and share your wisdom. Your knowledge. Your hope. Everyone experiences pain. Talk about how to confront it and embrace it.

Communicate with your family, your friends, and your loved ones what you learned about yourself in prison, and how you've changed. They may not know who you are. Or they may think you're the same person who hurt them before going to jail. Communication takes work. But it can yield peace and serenity in relationships. And if the words get stuck, if they just refuse to come out of your mouth, then write them down. A heartfelt note can work miracles. If you're sorry, write an apology. Writing allows you to carefully choose your words, think about them, and be sure it's exactly what you mean— without yelling and without hurtful accusations. It's nearly impossible to argue by letter. Sometimes difficult, painful issues can be resolved through letters.

⫷◈⫸

"Anybody know who the Quakers are?"

"Yeah, they make that stuff you eat for breakfast."

"Thanks," I said. "The Quakers developed the idea of the penitentiary in the 1800s. It was a vast improvement over the flogging and whipping that took place up until then. A penitentiary literally means a place to think, to reflect. The lessons learned, the wisdom gained while incarcerated, can be shared with others.

"Viktor Frankl wrote about how the loss he experienced gave him clarity about what was important to him, about what life meant. Nelson Mandela wrote about freedom and his long struggle to achieve it. Martin Luther King, Jr. wrote about injustice and inequality. Sometimes fighting for what you believe in lands you in jail. These are important, life-changing issues. Use the power of these concepts to communicate with others. When returning to society, organizations dedicated to reentry want to hear from you. Write to them about your experience. You could motivate and inspire others to succeed in reentry."

I went back to the chalkboard. Above the list of names of those who had been incarcerated, I wrote the word "epiphany." I turned to the class, now anxious for the go-back, all of us a day closer to going home. I asked, "Anybody know what an epiphany is?"

"It's when you curse at someone."

"It's something they write on your tombstone."

"Nah, nah, nah. It's something that happens in church."

"You're on the right track," I said. "It can happen in church. Hopefully, it happens before they engrave your tombstone."

I told the men that it's an "aha!" moment. A realization. Enlightenment—a moment when the entire arduous journey starts to make sense. Maybe you'll discover your mission in life. Maybe it's simply an insight as to why we all suffer.

An epiphany can occur in prison. It can change your life. And it can give you the strength you'll need during reentry. But, remember, real change takes work every single day. Change has to be your number one priority. Losing sight of your goal for one day, one moment, can cost you all the freedom you've worked so hard to achieve.

"I'll leave you with a few words from Viktor Frankl: 'The victim of a hopeless situation, facing a fate he cannot change, may rise above himself, may grow beyond himself, and by so doing, change himself.'

"This is the Transition Center. A transition is a change. It's all about change, guys."

Over the intercom, a correction officer announced, "On the go-back." As I collected my notes, the class filed out. One guy hung back, the one who had raised his hand to read "Letter from a Birmingham Jail."

"Let me get Dr. King's essay for you," I told him.

"Yo, that was good today. I got a lot out of that."

"Thanks, I like hearing that."

Sometimes I think I've finally found my mission in life.

CONTRIBUTORS

In addition to offering biographical information, the authors express their hopes and dreams for themselves and humanity, as well as gratitude to the special people in their lives.

Tamara Anderson

I am a native of the Pacific Northwest. Growing up, I benefited from a loving grandmother who compensated for some of my early setbacks as a child of a poorly equipped teenage mother and stepfather. I attended the Evergreen State College in Olympia, Washington, where I focused on philosophy, literature, and social science. After graduating, I began a career in nonprofit social services as a fundraiser in New York City, and I began writing fiction. On the surface, I seemed to be doing well. But my life always felt like a struggle with conflicting forces: the patterns of violence learned from my parents, a lack of support and financial resources, my acute awareness of injustice—personal and societal—and my love of art and literature. For a long time, struggling with these forces left me feeling trapped and hopeless about my future—so much so that I almost gave up my life. I'm grateful for the people, some of them virtual strangers, who stepped in when I desperately needed help. I'm grateful for my mother, who is now her true self—a sweet, kind, and generous person. I'm grateful for Prabu Vasan, a wonderful poet and outstanding human. And I'm grateful for the Dharma, which is always there.

Mattie Evans Belle

I was born and raised in Queens, New York, and am the middle child in a family of six. I am also the mother of one, and the grandmother of three. I enjoy music, reading, writing, and lately, exercising—nothing too strenuous, just a little yoga, and at least four to five miles a week on the treadmill or the track. I have been in the human services field for close to ten years and sincerely believe it to be my true vocation. My greatest contribution to life is assisting other people with theirs.

Shaun A. Bowen

I was born in Vermont and grew up in Maine. I eventually made my way to Syracuse, New York, where I will probably live upon my re-release in 2011. One of my major goals is to help people avoid making the same mistakes I made. And as someone who is in recovery, I hope to help people who have addictions. I enjoy reading (including psychology, comparative religion, history, philosophy, science), doing puzzles (especially sudoku—I'm addicted), writing short stories, watching movies, fishing, and spending nights at home—I'm sort of a homebody. A turning point in my life was returning to prison on a violation and losing contact with my son. That's when I realized I needed to enter a therapeutic program in order to dig deep and make sure that I didn't take prison home with me again. The other major turning point in my life was my submitting to God, my Higher Power.

Anthony Brown

In the absolute darkest period of my life, I discovered a guiding light through writing. What began as simple cathartic release quickly progressed into a fervent passion. Manuscripts were amassed, an audience was envisioned, and the quest for publication was begun. Today, this former *persona non grata* is CEO of Razorwriter Entertainment, author of *Razor Wire Love* (scheduled for release in 2010) and looking forward to paying my daughter's college tuition in a few years. I'm a late bloomer who is extremely proud of my growth. That's a feeling that I never could have schemed for, stolen, or swindled. I can be contacted at *anthonyjbrown79@yahoo.com*.

Robert Cepeda

I'm from the Bronx, New York. I have made mistakes in life, as we all have. But today I'm focusing on reaching for a life I've long dreamed of—working in film and animation.

I read all I can about filmmaking. Independent filmmakers like Tyler Perry have been an inspiration to me; they made me see that small, well-made films can make a difference. I'm thinking outside these prison walls to a better life.

Dean A. Faiello

Inspired by the squawk of seagulls and early morning espresso, I write. My essays have been published in *The Minnesota Review, Descant,* and *Stone Canoe.* I write creative nonfiction, fueled by the chaotic journey that led me to Attica Correctional Facility, where I work in the Transitional Services Center and prepare inmates for successful reentry into society. I thank the insanity of my life for being an inexhaustible fount of material.

Mansfield B. Frazier

I began seriously writing at age fifty, while serving a sentence in federal prison for manufacturing counterfeit credit cards, a career I pursued for close to thirty years. During my last incarceration, I wrote *From Behind the Wall: Commentary on Crime, Punishment, Race, and the Underclass.* The book was published the same month I was released for the final time, in April 1995. It became my passport to another life—a life in journalism.

I was a writer and editor at the *Cleveland Tab* newsmagazine, editor at the *Cleveland Call and Post,* and managing editor at *CityNews* before moving to cable television and freelance journalism. My work is now featured on the Internet on

CoolCleveland.com, and nationally on the *Daily Beast.* Now in the vanguard of the reentry movement, I serve on the Cuyahoga County Reentry Strategy Committee, and am editor and publisher of its newsletter, the *Reentry Advocate.* I am also the executive director of Neighborhood Solutions, a nonprofit organization that focuses on reentry issues. With a grant from the Department of Justice, my organization is producing a textbook on prisoner reentry for use at post-secondary institutions. I live in Cleveland with my wife, Brenda, and our two dogs. My hobbies are bicycling and gardening.

Bridget Jones

I am a native of Little Rock, Arkansas, a single mother of two, and an advocate for true prison reform. I have written several pieces and am completing my first novel. Born to a disabled mother, I made survival choices that landed me in prison. My prison experience and the murder of my older brother made me change the way I was living. I now use my life experiences to help uplift others. I am a motivational speaker on a range of topics, including these: single parenting, abused children, prison reform, and life skills. I am a Christian who understands the power of forgiveness and grace. My work never stops. You can contact me at *fruitfulpathways@aol.com.*

Delores Mariano

I was born in Los Angeles—yes, a real Californian. My ethnic heritage is rich, with roots in Prussia, Sicily, Germany, and, eight centuries back, Ethiopia. I have two daughters and a beautiful granddaughter, who is a toddler and a handful. My son died in 2008. My mother is in her late eighties and full of life. I've had medical problems and was pronounced dead twice in prison and once on the outside. I beat death so that I could make a positive difference for women who are beaten down inside prison walls. My passion is to find release and relief for women who are falsely imprisoned or imprisoned past their real release dates. I want to give them hope that they will have a tomorrow. Much love to all, and respect to those who will print the truth.

Esther Morales Guzman

I migrated to the United States from the beautiful state of Oaxaca, Mexico, in 1989; I was thirty years old. I was imprisoned in 2003 and released in 2008. I was deported to Tijuana, B.C., Mexico, where I became involved in the immigrant rights movement, including cooking for fundraisers, leafleting at the border, attending events, and managing a second-hand store that provided funds for a migrant women's shelter. After a five-year separation caused by my imprisonment, I was reunited with my fifteen- year-old daughter, Eliza, when she joined me in Mexico. Eliza eventually returned to the U.S. to attend school, and I decided to attempt to cross the border to join her. I was caught by the border patrol and sentenced to twenty-seven months in federal immigration detention for my activist work in the immigrant rights movement. I will be released in September 2010. I hope to establish myself in Tijuana so that I can be close to Eliza, who will soon be graduating from high school.

Tariq Mayo

I am an ex-drug dealer from Harlem, New York. I discovered my passion for print while incarcerated at Marcy Correctional Facility, in Marcy, New York—and I've never looked back. I am enrolled in a freelance-writing college correspondence course and am working on my first mainstream novel, a suspense thriller titled *Shooter.* I also write urban/hip-hop fiction under the colorful pseudonym Red Rocker. I received my associate of applied science degree in business management from Columbus State Community College in Ohio, and I was also in the Job Corps, where I received training in security, accounting, cabling, and business administration. I live in the Bronx.

Jonathan M. Petty

I was born and raised in Cleveland, Ohio, and have been writing and recording for more than eighteen years. Fooled by quick money and the glitz and glamour of the street life, my true talents were put on the back burner and left simmering due to my years of incarceration.

The biggest turning point in my life came when I called my father from prison when he was on his deathbed. His last words to me were, "You ain't shit, but a no-good hoodlum that will never be shit." Every time I pick up a pen, I repeat those words as motivation to be the best at whatever I do. As a rapper, I go by the moniker "The Chronic Boss" and have performed with my cousin, "Mr. Black Boob," at concerts around Cleveland. My goal is to share my mistakes with the younger generation so that they can soar instead of making the mistakes I made. My advice: Find your purpose, and push it like you would that bag on the block. Finally, I want to give a quick shout-out to my homies Gene, Boo, and Tae Smalls. Get at me.

John Ruzas

I was born in 1943 to Irish and Lithuanian parents, and grew up in Corona, Queens. I entered the carpenters union as an apprentice when I was eighteen, and remained in the construction trade until my arrest in 1974. After being found not guilty of the intentional murder of a New York state trooper, I escaped the death penalty but received a sentence of twenty-five years to life. In 1987, a neighborhood girl came back into my life and we were married in 1989. I am blessed with her continued love and that of four grown stepchildren, as well as nine grandchildren who think that Grandpa is a construction foreman building roads in Iraq. Writing has been a means of escape—my literary motto is, "I write because I can't fly"—and it has earned me awards. Over more than three decades, I have been a tutor in various state prisons; nothing gives me greater pleasure than watching an illiterate man become literate. After thirty-six years and eight parole board appearances, I will appear again in November 2011. Someday, I will stroll the length of Central Park with Sophia Loren. Of course, my wife will meet us at the end. That's the kind of Aquarian dreamer I am.

David Stephenson

I was born and raised in Texas. I didn't leave that state until after I graduated from medical school in San Antonio, in 1988. While the education I received to become a doctor was solid, it was nothing like the eye-opening experience of the past five years of incarceration. I'm moving back to Texas to get back on my feet, but I will be visiting my kids in New York at every opportunity. I hope to eventually be permanently reunited with them. I am blessed that they are still young and there is so much I can teach them about the world. I am formulating some entrepreneurial ideas (all perfectly legit, to be sure!) and will actively pursue them when I am released.

Tion Terrell

I grew up in a dysfunctional household in rural Doswell, Virginia. I was grossly neglected and subjected to physical, emotional, and sexual abuse; my adolescence was spent in foster homes, youth shelters, and other institutions. This set the stage for delinquency, incarceration, and recidivism. Despite my upbringing, my ambition and intelligence enabled me to attain high-level employment with several companies. This and other accomplishments gave me the confidence to continue striving for success after I was sentenced to ten years in prison in October 2000. Throughout my imprisonment, I educated myself, with the intention of fathering and leading a healthy family, owning successful businesses, becoming an author and poet, and founding a charity that provides educational and other opportunities to at-risk youth and the incarcerated. Already, I've earned awards for my poetry and nonfiction, and I've been sought by publishers of fiction across the country. My blog address is *supamansays.blogspot.com*.

Larry White

I am the community advocate and policy liaison for the Fortune Society's David Rothenberg Center for Public Policy. In this role I assist in the development and advancement of Fortune's criminal justice policy advocacy agenda. I'm also director of the Hope Lives for Lifers Project, which provides guidance and direction to incarcerated individuals serving life, long-term and life-without-parole sentences, and encourages them to live a purposeful and productive life in prison. During thirty-two years in prison, I served as chairman of a number of inmate-led reform organizations and developed empowerment programs designed to address, from a cultural perspective, the problems surrounding adjustment to prison. I was a primary advocate for offering college courses in prison, programs for the elderly, and community-sponsored study groups such as the Quaker-sponsored Alternative to Violence Program.

The effect of my advocacy can be measured by the degree of organization among the incarcerated in New York State, as well as among their families and supporters in the communities most impacted by high incarceration rates.

Melvin Wright

I was born on January 16, 1954, in Atlanta, Georgia. My goal is to educate and train teenagers about the pitfalls of experimenting with sex and drugs. I want to teach them how to give seminars to their peers that include visual aids depicting real-life situations. I have a strong desire to save the young from the harsh realities I experienced growing up.

Editors' Bios

Sheila R. Rule is founder of Resilience Multimedia, a publishing company that seeks to present a fairer image of the incarcerated, the formerly incarcerated, and their loved ones. A journalist at *The New York Times* for more than thirty years before retiring from that newspaper, she was led to publishing by her love of books and her respect for the power of stories.

Marsha R. Rule (Marsha R. Leslie) is a writer and editor for UW Medicine, University of Washington, Seattle. She edited *The Single Mother's Companion: Essays and Stories by Women* (Seal Press, 1994) and contributed to *The Black Womens' Health Book* (Seal Press, 1990, 1994). She lives in Seattle.

Order Form

Ordering Method:

Telephone: Call 877-267-2303 toll free.
Have your credit card ready.

Email: *resiliencemultimedia@verizon.net*

Postal: Resilience Multimedia, Dept. B,
511 Avenue of the Americas, Suite 525
New York, NY 10011

Online: *www.thinkoutsidethecell.org*

All books are $14.95 plus shipping:
$3.50 (book rate; delivery speed varies)
$5.75 (priority mail; approx. 1–3 days)

New York residents, please add 8.875% sales tax.
Discount schedule for bulk orders is available upon request.

Number of Copies Requested:

_____ *Love Lives Here, Too: Real-Life Stories about Prison Marriages and Relationships*

_____ *Counting the Years: Real-Life Stories about Waiting for Loved Ones to Return Home from Prison*

_____ *The Hard Journey Home: Real-Life Stories about Reentering Society after Incarceration*

_____ *Think Outside the Cell: An Entrepreneur's Guide for the Incarcerated and Formerly Incarcerated*

Name:_____

Address:_____

City: _____ State:_____Zip: _____

Daytime phone: _____

Email address: _____

Payment: ❑ Check payable to Resilience Multimedia

❑ Credit card: ❑ Visa ❑ MasterCard ❑ Amex ❑ Discover

Card number: _____ Exp. Date: _____

Name on card:_____